The Joy
of Winning

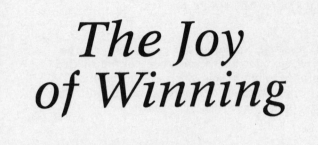

The Joy of Winning

MICHAEL BEER

MERCURY

First published in 1990
by the Mercury Books Division of
W.H. Allen & Co. Plc
Sekforde House, 175–9 St John Street, London EC1V 4LL

Set in Concorde by Phoenix Photosetting, Chatham
Printed and bound in Great Britain by
Butler & Tanner Ltd, Frome, Somerset

British Library Cataloguing in Publication Data

Beer, Michael, *1926–*
  The joy of winning.
  1. Salesmanship
  I. Title
  685.8′5

ISBN 1–85252–081–7

CONTENTS

1 Introduction 1

2 Knowledge 11

3 Killer Instinct 27

4 The success, the failure, and the Non-success 41

5 Self-renewal 51

6 Destination 59

7 Self-reliance 73

8 Excuses, excuses 81

9 Pride of Performance 89

10 Specialisation 95

11 Self-confidence 99

12 Are you better than your score? 107

13 Lazy or idle? 121

14 Retreat to victory – the easiest way to win 131

15 Communication 135

16   Recognition   143
17   Attitude   153
     Index   163

This is the book
I have always wanted
to write.
I dedicate it to
every Non-success
in the world.
May you know – and reach –
your destinations.

Michael Beer

1
INTRODUCTION

Who is running your life?

This is the most important question anyone has ever asked you.

Who is running your life?

All right, since no one has ever asked you this question before, since I have thrown it at you without any warning, you may need some time to think about it.

There are only three possible answers. No, in fact there is a fourth answer. It is: 'That is none of your damn' business.' You could try that one if you like, but it won't get you very far. Also, it's wrong; it *is* my business. You have made it my business by starting to read this, and if you don't want me in your life then stop reading now. If you go on reading you are inviting me to stick my nose into your business – and your life.

Who is running your life? Here are the three answers:

1. 'I am. I am running my life. I make the decisions. Naturally, I am helped when I need it by friends and family; I don't live in

[1]

> Success is just a matter of luck. Ask any failure.
>
> *Earl Wilson*

a vacuum. But I decide when or if I need that help. I know where I'm going, I know how to get there, I know how far I am along the road. *I* am running my life.'

Fine! Well, you certainly don't need me, but who knows, we may meet along the way some time. In the meantime, congratulations on having your life so well planned and organised; you probably know that you are in a very fortunate minority. I would wish you good luck, except that you would tell me that you don't need it, and you would be right.

2. 'Other people. Other people are running my life. I don't seem to have any say in it and haven't had since I was at school. My father decided where I should go to school, my mother decided what I should wear there, my teachers decided what subjects I should take, my friends decided what games we should play, my uncle decided what business I should go into, my wife decided what size family we should have, my children decided where we should go for holidays, and the odds are good that when I die the undertaker will decide what my tombstone will look like. Whatever it looks like the inscription should read: "This man's life was run by other people".'

Well, before I commiserate with you, before we cry on each other's shoulders, we have to recognise that there are two subdivisions to answer number 2:

2(a). 'Other people run my life *and I like it that way*. I coast through life and that's the way I want it to be. Other people can make the important decisions for me. Other people can wind me up and point me in the right direction every morning and I'll go happily clicking through the day. If you think that this is a terrible way to live you should try it some time and you may find that it isn't bad at all. I don't have a worry in the world, I'm in a non-stress situation, and I shall probably outlive all my contemporaries. I have enough. I have my family, my friends, my stamp-collecting, squash, bird-spotting, fretwork or fishing and I am content. My life is run by other people, and I hope they never stop.'

Fine! Well, you certainly don't need me, and I doubt that we shall meet again. I would wish you good luck, except that you would tell me that you don't need it, and you would be right.

2(b). 'Other people run my life *and I hate it*. I really do hate it and I should love more than anything else to change it. The trouble is that I have got into a habit-pattern of *expecting* other people to make the important decisions in my life. At work I expect my boss to order me around, to tell me what to do, how to do it and when to stop doing it. At home I expect my family to tell me that now is the time to buy a new car and that this is the one to buy; that we should move to a bigger/ smaller house which is closer to/further from town.

'Other people run my life and I hate it but I don't know how to change.'

All right, I hear you and I congratulate you for being perceptive enough to understand your situation and for being courageous enough to come right out with it. Keep your courage; help is at hand.

3. 'I don't know who is running my life. At times it seems that I do have a hand in my destiny, if that's not too pompous a word for one life. Then fate seems to chuck a spanner in the works and everything grinds to a halt or simply turns into a

[3]

mess. I don't know what to do about this and I also don't know who is running my life – it probably isn't *me*.'

An honest man – and one of a large majority. When Thoreau wrote that 'The mass of men lead lives of quiet desperation,' he was looking straight at our unhappy friend.

Well, you have had a little time to think about it, so again I ask you: *Who is running your life?*

Naturally, when we talk of running our lives we recognise that no single person is free to do as he pleases. We are restricted by the law of the land from the legal point of view, and by our own personal code of ethics from the moral point of view. So we don't steal our neighbours' chickens, which would be illegal, and we don't steal their wife or husband, which would be immoral. Without these restrictions (and thank God we have them) – Chaos, but within these bounds, are you doing what you want to do?

You can run your own life. You can take charge. You can decide where you are going and how you want to get there. Yes, you really can.

– And let us stop right here and sit back and admit something.

You have heard it before, haven't you? You have read 'Success' books before. You know the ones I mean – the rags to riches stories. 'I was born without a father or mother, in a ghetto, with a mortgage, a cleft palate and a paternity suit against me, and now I'm Chairman of Consolidated Amalgamated Megacorp!' – that sort of thing. There are plenty of them around; the shelves of bookstores groan with the titles of books written by people who, they claim, were at the bottom and are now at the top.

What is wrong with these books? There is no doubt of their sincerity; read them and it is obvious that the writers mean every word they say. There is no doubt of their truth; many of

[4]

the authors are household names, famed far and wide for their achievements. They are indeed the successes they claim to be.

Oh, yes, you have read them. You have picked them off the racks in supermarkets, ordered them through the mail, borrowed them from the public libraries. You started reading eagerly, keen to learn the magic which made these people great. Surely there would be something in these pages which you could use to fulfil your own destiny! What happened, as you went through page after page, consumed chapter after chapter until you had read the last word and closed the book?

Well, if you are a normal, average sort of person what happened was that you put down the book feeling worse than when you picked it up.

How do you like that? Here is a book which is supposed to encourage, motivate and spur you on to a better life, and all it has done is to make you profoundly depressed.

Now, why should this be? Here is the story about a person who has overcome deficiencies, disabilities and adversity and has emerged stronger than before to triumph over, in many cases, the most shocking bludgeonings of chance. Surely it should inspire you, to read of these heroic and successful struggles?

It didn't inspire you. It depressed you. Reading these sagas made you feel worse, not better, and when you think that you probably plunked down some hard cash to buy the book you may feel that you have been ripped off.

But again, why the negative feelings from what after all is a very positive story? The reason is simple, and it is what is wrong with all the 'Success' books. It is this: you are a normal, average sort of person – *and those books are written by supermen*.

That's the answer. You read the books in the hope that you could in some way relate to the authors, that just possibly you could follow in their footsteps and tread the same road that they trod on their way to success. You finished reading and realised that you couldn't do the things those people did, you

[5]

couldn't attempt the heights which they scaled or reach the goals which they achieved. You are an ordinary mortal; they stand with the gods.

How this book is different

This is a different 'Success' book. This is not an account of how Michael Beer clawed his way to the top from abject poverty and, in spite of having been left as a baby outside the Mission door in the snow, rose to become the confidant of Royalty and Heads of State. In the first place I'm not the product of a dramatically deprived family and I don't know any Princes or Premiers, and secondly, although I do relate some personal experiences, this book isn't about me at all.

However, while we are on the subject, let's get me over so that we can get on to the important things:

You are reading the words of John Average. I have never been so good or so bad as to be interesting; medium is the story of my life. At school I was always half-way down the list of marks, I was second team cricket and third team football, first reserve for the swimming squad, didn't quite make the athletics side, class monitor but not house prefect, corporal in the cadet corps but not sergeant. In the army I wasn't promoted but I managed to stay out of detention barracks. The cleverest thing I ever did was to read a map better than my troop leader and get us back to camp before dark; the worst thing was to get fined five days' pay for having a dirty tommy-gun.

Even my golf handicap is medium; at 12 I am better than a rabbit, worse than a tiger. Mr Average.

As it happens, I do have a talent which has allowed me to make a living while I pursue my lifetime hobby, and it is this hobby which is my authority for writing this book.

[6]

The hobby? An enthusiastic study of the Winner. I have always been fascinated by what makes a person successful. It doesn't matter what field of endeavour it is – business, sport, the arts, politics – what is it that makes *that* person reach the summit while his contemporaries fall by the wayside?

My job is training, specifically in the disciplines of sales and management, and one of the spin-offs of the job is a free look at the men and women who are busy making successes of themselves. I work with people who have only just started on the first rung of the ladder of success, as well as those who are well on their way up it, and even a few who have reached the top of their own personal Matterhorn.

Then, of course, I also meet those who have got as far as they are ever going to get. I see those who haven't any chance of even starting the climb. Finally, and most unhappily, I find the ones who are on the way down.

I work with them all, I look for what makes them tick. A long time ago it dawned on me that there was a definite *pattern* in the philosophy and the performance of the winner.

Yes, there is a *Pattern of Winning*, and it is this pattern which you and I are going to study in these pages.

It doesn't take a superman

What you will come to realise, and it is the best piece of good news that you will ever get, is that the successful person, the Winner, *is not a superman*. He does nothing which the average person cannot do. He has nothing which the average person does not have. His achievements are not based on any unusual intelligence or aptitude. He is an ordinary person, and that is the truth.

Now, let's not be silly here. I don't know about you but I have always been irritated by those people who tell you that anyone can do anything. You know them, the 'What the mind can conceive the body can achieve' characters. Who do they think they are fooling? Three examples, so that we don't insult each other's intelligence with nonsense:

You may decided to win the Gold in the hundred yards sprint at the next Olympics, but you won't make it if you have the figure of a Sumo wrestler; for certain achievements you need certain *physical* characteristics.

You may decide to become Driver of the Year in next year's Formula One motor racing, but if you have bad hand–eye co-ordination and the reflexes of a three-toed sloth then all you are going to do is write yourself off against the safety fence; for certain achievements you need certain *inherent* characteristics.

You may decide that you will become a computer genius, but apparently the computer pundits have specific tests which will quickly tell you whether or not you are ever likely to be at home in the higher realms of computer technology. This has nothing to do with intelligence, it has to do with the way your mind works, and if it doesn't work in a special way the computer people are not going to be very interested in you; for certain achievements you need certain *mental* characteristics.

So, in certain fields certain basics are required and without these only a fool even attempts to succeed in them. A corollary here – there are of course many people who do have the right physical or mental characteristics to succeed in a certain job or under-taking but who will never succeed at it, and the reasons for their failures will form an intriguing, if tragic, part of our studies.

So, whether you are reading this in order to gather some of the secrets of success or whether you are simply fascinated, as I am, by what it is that makes the winner, let us start with the axiom that we are talking about ordinary people. *It doesn't take a superman.*

> There is only one success – to be able to spend your life in your own way.
>
> *Christopher Morley*

Yes, there is a Pattern of Winning. There is nothing especially mystical or abstruse about it, but so far as I know, no one has tried to put it on paper before. What you may find interesting is that the pattern is valid no matter what the winner chooses as his or her particular calling, business or activity. Be it professional ice-hockey, statesmanship, merchant banking, chess, *haute couture* or industrial chemistry, the winner does the things, thinks the things and *is* the things that all other winners do, think and are.

Which came first?

Wait a minute. We have a chicken-or-egg situation here. Is Charlie a winner because he follows a certain pattern, or does he follow that pattern because he is a winner? Important question; depending on the answer, half the reason for our getting together could fall away.

I am convinced that the chicken came first. People become winners because of what they do and think and are. If this is so then it must follow that anyone can become a winner, so long as he does and thinks and is the things that the winners do and think and are.

What are these things? What is the Pattern of Winning? We are about to find out, but remember that while we may look at some examples of extraordinary deeds, exploits and achievements, there is nothing here which can't be done by ordinary people; there would be no point in my writing this book if that were not true. *You don't have to be a superman.*

2
KNOWLEDGE

... Or, *'Gimme another thousand years and I'll have this taped.'*

The very first characteristic of the winner is this: he knows more than other people do.

Now, this may not be a very exciting piece of news to anyone who wants a quick and easy ticket to success. Perhaps

> We do not know one-millionth of one per cent about anything.
>
> *Thomas Alva Edison*

I should have started with one of the more dramatic characteristics of the winner, but that would have been a cop-out because this one is perhaps the most basic of all. The true professional in any field simply *knows*.

He doesn't know it all, of course. I was giving a talk to a group of managers in the pharmaceutical business, and it happened that the chief chemist of the company was sitting in. Partly for the shock effect I threw a statement at the group: 'There is not one single person in this room who knows enough about the products of this company.' Now bear in mind that the chemist had been responsible for creating and developing some of the drugs in the product range of the company, and in the circumstances my remark may have seemed to be lacking in tact.

I didn't expect it to go over with resounding applause, and certainly from the expressions on the faces of the delegates they were not very impressed with the statement. I saw some of them looking sideways to see how the chemist was taking it. He was taking it pretty well, since he was the only one in the room who was nodding his head. He knew that what I had said, even put as it was in a brutal and perhaps offensive way, was true. He agreed that he didn't know enough about his product range.

And there is another extension of this characteristic of the winner. Even though he knows more than other people, he also knows that it isn't enough, and he is constantly *un*satisfied – not so much *dis*satisfied – with the extent of his knowledge. You see, the mediocrity says: 'I know enough about my job. I know more than the people outside my business, and that's enough; I'm not a college professor, I'm not engaged in original research; I'm a practical person, and I have a good, sound practical knowledge. It's enough.'

The winner says: 'I don't know enough. I may just possibly have known enough yesterday, but this is today, and more has happened since yesterday. I must keep up. If I want to stay ahead I have to keep moving simply to stay in the same place. If I stop I fall behind.'

I have a friend who, until he retired, was an ophthalmic surgeon. He was so good that medical men sent their patients to him from all over the place. I say 'until he retired' but the truth is that nobody will let him retire, and he is still asked to read papers all over the world. When he was in practice he was always booked up for months in advance.

All of which is quite interesting when you realise that he didn't know his job. Every two years he would down tools and go back to school. I once asked him why he found this necessary at his level of success, when most people in his field found that they could get by with reading the medical journals and attending the occasional seminar. He said: 'Oh, I'm still an apprentice at my trade.' He wasn't being falsely modest or coy, he meant what he said.

So – the winner knows more, but even more important than that, he doesn't think it's enough. Never is it enough.

When I started in the training business I was in a fortunate position, because I had all the answers to all the training problems in the world. Now, some years down the road I seem to have lost all the answers and in fact I don't even know some of the questions, but at least I know that I don't know, which is a great help. Awareness of your ignorance is the first step towards knowledge.

Know your enemy!

However, none of the knowledge we have been talking about so far means anything at all unless we have another type of knowledge along with it. This second type of knowledge puts the first type in perspective and makes it meaningful and useful. What is it? An example will help.

I was sitting in my office one day counting my blessings and curses when a young man burst in. He was as nervous as a nun in a nightclub; shaking, sweating, and when he started to speak, stuttering.

'M-m-may I have t-t-ten minutes of your time, sir?' he said. He may have thought that he was smiling but the rictus on his face looked like the corpse of a man who had died three days ago.

'Sit down,' I said. He looked ready to fall down anyway, and I thought he might as well get off his feet one way or another.

'I'm a – I'm a salesman,' he volunteered.

I would never have guessed, I thought. I said, 'Okay, sit down.'

'I'm a – I'm a *life insurance* salesman,' he gulped. 'I hope that doesn't offend you?'

Wow, I thought. Now, that's a real assertive, macho way to start a sales call. 'No, it doesn't offend me,' I assured him. 'I believe in life insurance. Sit down.'

It wasn't as easy as that; he had one more thing to get off his chest. 'I'm a *brand-new* life insurance salesman,' he said. 'I just came out of our training school yesterday. You – you are my first sales call, sir!'

I thought, hear the man, dear St Jude. A virgin, straight-out-of-the-box salesman, and he has the curse of a twelve-footed troll on him because he picks a sales trainer as his first prospect. 'Well, you have to start somewhere,' I said. 'For openers, why don't you sit down?'

He finally did find a chair with his bottom. 'We – we have a marvellous new policy that I would like to show you, sir,' he said, less nervous now that it seemed that I was not going to cut his throat or dip him in boiling oil. 'May I show you?'

I said, 'Show me.'

He pulled out a pad and pencil and drew the beginnings of a simple graph:

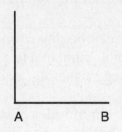

'Now, sir,' he said. 'Let us say that A is your age now, today, and B is your age at sixty-five. All right?'

It did seem to me that A and B were rather close together – perhaps I wasn't looking my best that day – but I didn't quibble. My new-found friend added a 'C' – to the graph:

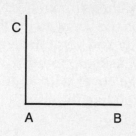

'Now, let us say that C is the total amount of insurance cover you need right now. Okay?' I nodded. He frowned in deep concern. 'The trouble, sir, is that that amount of insurance costs a fortune in premiums.'

'Tell me about it,' I agreed.

His face brightened. 'We have a solution! Do you know what we do?'

I said, 'No; tell me what you do.'

'We sell you *half* the amount of insurance!' He added another line D to his graph, half-way between A and C. He raised a hand to stop any complaint from me. 'You will say, sir, that it won't help you to have only half the amount of cover, not so?' Pressed, I admitted that I was now filled with foreboding at being only half covered.

He had good news to calm my fears. 'We sell you a *with-profit* policy,' he said. 'So that by the time you turn sixty-five it has risen to the full amount!' I opened my mouth to speak but again his raised hand forestalled me. 'But you want the cover now, not at sixty-five!' I conceded it freely; I did want the cover now. His smile was pure triumph as he quickly added two more lines to the graph:

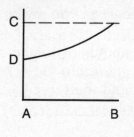

'So, we give you very cheap insurance to fill the gap between C and D. It gets less as the years go by, the profits policy gets more as the years go by and what have you got?'

'What have I got?' I asked obediently.

'You've got twice the cover with a little more than half the premiums! How do you like that, sir?'

'I like it!'

'You do?'

'Oh, I do, I do!'

'How much can I sell you, then?'

I hated to kill the euphoria. 'Nothing. Not a penny.'

He was thunderstruck. 'Why not, if you like it so much?'

I said, 'I like it so much I bought it from another insurance company, five years ago.'

He shook his head at my ignorance. 'I'm afraid that's quite impossible, sir. You couldn't have bought it from any other company. That's my company's policy, exclusive to us.'

I said, 'My friend, that's any company's policy. You have simply added reducing term to with-profit whole life, and any company can do that.'

Well, he walked out of my office a broken man; I had ruined his whole day and, for all I know, his whole career in life insurance.

I have never forgotten that man and I have set down this example in some detail because it makes my point better than anything else I could say. Think of him – he had just graduated from the College of Knowledge of his life insurance company – and he knew nothing whatever about life insurance. 'Oh, but of course he did!' comes the objection. 'Why, he explained his policy in detail! How can you say he knew nothing about insurance?'

He knew nothing about insurance *because he did not know what else was available in the market-place.* He did not know his enemy, and therefore what he knew about his own product was worthless.

[16]

There it is, the second area of knowledge. You know your job? You are aware of your own strengths and weaknesses? Fine, but you don't operate alone in your own galaxy; you have opposition, adversaries, competitors. Know them!

The winner spends inordinate amounts of time in learning about his enemies. It doesn't matter what he is or what he does, he finds out about the person in the opposite trenches. Examples:

Before the big election the professional politician goes over the opposing candidate's record with an electron microscope. How did he vote on that crucial piece of legislation? What is his personal life like? How much money does he have and how did he get it? He is vociferous about the need for a strong defence force but he keeps very quiet about pollution; what vested interests are behind his stance here? (Lord knows, I don't approve of this sort of thing, but clean politics is a contradiction in terms, and this *happens*).

Before the big fight the boxer spends hours watching videos of his opponent's recent fights. Has the media so glorified his right hook that he has begun to believe that it is omnipotent? Is this guy the exception to the rule 'Box a fighter and fight a boxer'? Why is he so protective of his left side?

Before the test match the opening bowler practises until dark, pitching balls to the exact spot where they will pop up just outside the off-stump. The opening batsman on the other side has one weakness only – he can't resist slashing at that particular ball, and the bowler is making sure that he will fall victim to the waiting hands of the slips.

Before the football game the coach makes good use of his overhead projector to plot counter-strategies to known formations of the opposition.

In business, marketing companies employ special staff to investigate opposition packaging, pricing and promotions;

market research companies go to extraordinary lengths to find out why people buy competitive products.

The winner knows his enemy. He knows his weaknesses, surely, and he makes the best use of those weaknesses. The tennis player endlessly hitting into his opponent's forehand knows that he glories in his backhand but that he has a tendency when tired to put forehand drives straight into the net.

But the winner also knows his enemy's strengths. He searches out these strengths because the knowledge will give him confidence, not fear. Here is an interesting paradox. When you know exactly how *good* your opponent is, you also know his *limitations*. It is not knowledge of the enemy's strength which puts fear in the heart of anyone who is about to meet him in mortal combat, it is *ignorance*. 'How good is he really? What powers, talents and skills does he have which I know nothing about?' That is the soil in which fear grows.

All of which reminds me that I am playing golf tomorrow with a friend who loves nothing better than to take my money. He is a tough competitor, but while his strength is his distance off the tee, the course we are playing tomorrow is unprotected from the south-east wind, and my barometer is rising fast. This means that the south-easter will be blowing hard across the course, and his long, high drives will be blown into places where civilised man has never set foot. Also, he hates short, lofted shots, and that course abounds with problems around the greens which require delicate little lofted wedges.

Any amount he wants to bet, I'll cover it.

Does it take a superman to know your enemy? I know a man who looks as much like Superman as Peter Rabbit does. He was a salesman in the copying division of a company where I worked. We sold a good machine but morale among the sales people was low because everyone knew that an opposition company was on the point of bringing a new machine on to

> Man's business is to know for the sake of living, not to live for the sake of knowing.
>
> *Frederic Harrison*

the market, with features which made it a real breakthrough in the copier industry.

At a sales meeting one salesman voiced the fears of the group. 'Just how good is this thing?' he asked. 'Do we have any chance at all of selling against it?'

The sales manager nodded. He said, 'Yes, I think so, but we are trying to get more information about it and we should have it soon.'

At this point our hero put up his hand. He said, 'I have the information right now.'

This statement got a horse-laugh from the sales team and a look of irritation from the sales manager. He said, 'Tommy, shut up. This is too serious a business to play games. Sit down.'

The marketing director, who had been sitting silent at the back of the room, said, 'Hold it, Dave. Tommy, what do you mean, you have the information?'

Tommy stood up. In his hands were letters, brochures, manuals. He said, 'I wrote to the company's head office overseas as a private individual and said I was interested in their new concept of copying, and could they let me have some information. They sent me all this stuff. I've done a sort of product comparison with our copier on this sheet here – '

Picture the scene. The dead silence from the group, the sales manager not knowing where to look, and Tommy saying that from the comparison he had done it seemed that the new copier was indeed a good one but look here – there are some aspects of ours which actually beat it.

From then on the marketing director acted as though he

and Tommy were the only people in the room, with Tommy showing him the sales literature, the two of them discussing it, and finally the two of them leaving the room with the marketing director's arm over Tommy's shoulder and his saying brusquely: 'You guys carry on with your meeting.'

It is hardly surprising to learn that Tommy was promoted to area manager two months later. The point of the story is *that Tommy did nothing that anyone else couldn't do*. All he did was ask himself a few simple questions.

1. *How good is the new product?* Answer: I don't know.

2. *Who does know?* Answer: the people who make it.

3. *How can I get to know what they know?* Answer: Why not ask them?

Does it take a superman? Never, but it did take just a touch of thought. No great intelligence, talent or perception, just sitting back and putting three brain cells in a row. Sometimes I think that the best way to handle most of the problems in life is to start by asking ourselves three simple questions:

What is happening right now?

How do I want it changed?

What is the simplest way to change it?

I come back to our first axiom, that it doesn't take a superman. Tommy was an ordinary person and he did something very

---

Knowledge is of two kinds. We know a subject ourselves, or we know where to find information on it.

Samuel Johnson

---

ordinary – which made the rest of the group look like a bunch of twits.

And there's a danger. Since most people are not running their own lives, when you do take a hand in running yours you sometimes show up the people around you. Your friends and associates may not care for being made to look half-witted. You won't do it deliberately, it just happens. The traditional, time-honoured cry of the also-ran is: 'Why didn't I think of that?'

And please remember when he says this that he is not talking about the invention of the semi-conductor or the discovery of DNA and the double helix or the concept of the expansion theory of the universe. He doesn't bewail the fact that it was someone else, not he, who created the turbo-charger or the microwave or the compact disc. He's not uptight about the complex and highly technical ideas that have made people rich and famous; it's the simple things that people have done that bug him.

Like wanting to know about a copying machine and writing to the people who make it.

Of course, knowing something, thinking of something or deciding something and not acting on that something is like buying or being given a screwdriver or bicycle or umbrella and never using them. There was a group of clerks in a department of a firm, and during a particularly busy time one of them was heard to complain about the duplication of effort it required to complete two forms. 'They could easily combine them into one form,' she said crossly. 'But don't hold your breath for the management of *this* place to do anything as sensible as that.' Some of the other women agreed that it was unlikely that management would ever get so smart.

One of the women said nothing. Instead she took the two forms home and worked on them, and a week later the office manager walked in and announced to the department that Helen had conceived an excellent way to reduce the paperwork of the office, and she waved Helen's revised form at the group. Helen, she said, was getting a bonus for the idea.

Monica was outraged. 'Hey, that was *my* idea!' she said. 'I mentioned it weeks ago!'

The office manager turned a sceptical eye on Monica. 'Yes? Then why didn't you do something about it? We need doers in this office, not talkers.'

Monica was furious with Helen for stealing her idea, but in fact it wasn't her idea any more. She had thought of it, looked it over, mentioned it, and thrown it away. Helen had picked it up out of the gutter and done something about it.

More? Five junior managers in a company. Within a year one of them will be promoted to middle management. Everyone knows this, everyone also knows that the lucky one has not yet been picked. Each one is doing a competent job and there seems to be little to choose between them.

Then the Chief Executive of the parent company comes over to this country from Paris – did I mention that this was a subsidiary of a French company? – and he has a casual chat with each of the five aspirants. Not a formal interview, just shooting the breeze. The great man is first astonished, then amused, and finally impressed when one of the candidates for promotion addresses him in French. Not very fluent French, it's true, but French. He had been taking French lessons, had joined the *Alliance Français*, had started reading French books.

I'm sure you can write the script for the reactions of the

DEFINITION OF A WINNER: He took the trouble.

---

other four managers when our young polyglot got the promotion. 'Bootlicking.' 'A cheap trick.' 'If the big boss didn't realise why Peter learnt French then he's a big fool.'

Fairly obvious reactions from the also-rans, the men in the mob, but let's stay for a moment with the last comment. Do we really think that the great man from over the water believed that Peter had learnt French because he was entranced by the beauty of the language or because he wished to read Voltaire or Racine in the original? Of course not; he had not gained his exalted position without shedding a few illusions along the way. He knew that Peter had ploughed through the *plume de ma tante* for one reason only – so that he could address senior executives of the parent company in their own tongue. He was 'First astonished, then *amused*, and finally impressed.'

Oh, yes, Monsieur le Chef was amused, but which of the five interviews do you think he remembered when the time came to discuss the promotion? Right; a very ordinary, average sort of bloke who had laid out a few pounds on some French lessons.

What were Peter's friends doing while he was wondering why a table should be feminine? We don't know, but they could simply have been wasting their time.

Whoa! Hold everything! We could start an argument about those last three words which could turn into a full-scale war. We could also spend the rest of the book on them but instead let's just toss some ideas around. We have to do it some time and now is as good a time as any.

This is one characteristic where we average types differ from the superpeople. Read the biographies of the titans, those giants of commerce who bestride the narrow world like a Colossus, and what do you find? In most cases these whizz-bangs haul themselves out of bed at five in the morning straight into an ice-cold shower and by six they are at their desks. They keep going without a break until eight in the evening and then take home a briefcase the size of a cabin trunk and work at their desks at home until after midnight. Every few months a woman, whom they dimly recognise as the person they walked up an aisle with, puts her head in the door and says: 'Darling, I thought you might like to know that our daughter's wedding was a great success. Mother died, the doctor said it was for the best, and the wreath that your secretary sent in your name was in excellent taste. I saw my lawyer today and our divorce should be through in three months. Don't sit up too late, and don't forget to take your pills.'

That's how the Moguls operate. They do not waste one single second of their time. Do we want to be like that? The hell with it, who needs it?

I *like* wasting time. I actually enjoy it. A few more paragraphs of this and I am going to switch off my typewriter, grab my three-wood and five-iron, and go down to the practice range and bang off a hundred balls. Now, that will be a complete waste of time. They call it a practice range but what I shall be doing won't be practice because practice is supposed to make perfect, and all the thousands of balls I have banged off have not made the slightest difference to my standard of skill at the game. It isn't even exercise; it doesn't do my cardio-vascular system the least bit of good, and all I have to show for it are some callouses on the right places on my hands and that familiar pain in my lower back which my doctor warned me about. Neither of which is any use to me and the whole hour will be a complete waste of time.

What makes it different from the way that other people waste time is that it is deliberate, timed, and calculated. What is unforgivable tragedy is *mindless* waste of time. How many times have you sat through a television programme and at the end said, 'Well, that was a sorry waste of time!' Understand me: I'm not talking about something you looked forward to and then found to be a disappointment. No, here is a series, shall we say, or a serial or, heaven help us, a chat show, which you have suffered through before and not enjoyed. It comes on the screen and, damn it all, you sit through it, knowing that you will get nothing from it. Now *that* is a mortal sin, a terrible waste of time, and the winner never commits it.

Waste your time! Go ahead, do it! Smell the flowers along the way. Nothing in these pages says that you have to work eighteen hours a day for nearly half a century so that you can retire and look forward to ten years of not knowing what to do, and having even that cut short by an exploding aneurism which drops you stone dead in the middle of a yawn. Waste your time; it belongs to you to do with as you please. Waste it, but do it deliberately. Fling roses, roses, riotously with the throng – but then walk away from the throng and learn about the rival copier, fuse the two forms together to make one, conjugate a few French verbs. The throng will run out of roses to fling and look around for something else to waste their time on; you will be winning.

Knowledge, and it is knowledge which has concerned us in this chapter, is power; or so the saying goes. Like most sayings it has been hallowed by time and to question it verges on blasphemy. I do question it. Knowledge by itself isn't power. The academics in all the universities in the world hold in their heads all the knowledge in the world, but they have no power at all. KNOWLEDGE WITH ACTION IS POWER. You will *use* the knowledge you gain and it will make you a winner. But you need the knowledge first.

3
KILLER INSTINCT

One of the most simple and most obvious characteristics of the winner is – he loves to win. This is so simple and obvious that I wouldn't even have bothered to record it except that it has an important corollary: if he loves to win then it follows that *he hates to lose*.

And the immediate reaction to that is that if he hates to lose he must be a bad sport, and the hell with him.

This is not so. Hating to lose has nothing to do with bad sportsmanship. You don't accept this? You believe that good sportsmanship means being a 'good loser'?

Well, let's define our terms here. The so-called 'good loser' is surely one who graciously acknowledges that he was beaten

> You must be the anvil or the hammer.
>
> *Goethe*

fairly and squarely. He recognises his opponent's superiority – *at that time, at that place*. He ungrudgingly congratulates him. Now, anyone who conforms to all this is surely a 'good loser', right? But he can still hate to lose, and if he is a true winner then he does.

A beautiful example of this happened at Wimbledon in 1984 when Andrea Jaeger blew Chris Evert out of the Women's Singles. Now, some time before that event Ms Evert had been interviewed on television and I clearly remember her conceding that while money was no longer a factor in her career, still when she walked on to a tennis court she played every game as though her life depended on it because, she said, 'I hate to lose.'

As it happened, the night before the Jaeger–Evert match Chris had suffered from a severe gastric problem which necessitated medical treatment and which cost her a sleepless night. After the match the press brought up the tummy trouble she had had, and how easy it would have been for her to go along with this excellent (and perfectly valid) reason for her defeat.

Not my Chrissie (she has always been my personal heroine in tennis rather than some of her bionic opponents). She firmly and finally squashed this easy excuse and put it on record that she had been beaten by a better opponent, at that time, at that place.

The winner loves to win and hates to lose, and the money, the prizes, the plaudits and the kudos seem to have very little to do with it. I was running a sales training clinic in the island of Mauritius for a marketing company, and the management had taken the opportunity of having the whole team together to hand out the prizes for selling excellence for the past year. One salesman, the crackerjack of the team, walked off with the lion's share of the loot, and it was worthwhile loot, too; holidays in Hong Kong, state of the art hi-fi – that sort of thing.

Now it so happened that that afternoon he had persuaded me to play nine holes of golf with him. I wasn't all that keen because the course attached to the hotel was a primitive affair with the green like fairways, fairways like rough, and rough like Tarzan country, and with my standard of golf I need all the help I can get from the course. However since he was, after all, a top salesman he sold me on the idea of playing, and we teed off after he suggested that we have a golf ball on the game. It turned out to be as tight a game as one could wish, and he had to sink a five-foot putt to win on the last hole.

That night after the prize-giving my opponent was being congratulated on his achievements over the past year. He smiled politely at the nice things that management said about him. It wasn't until I came up and add my felicitations that he came alive. Then he banged me on the back and relived every shot of our golf match, and as a dramatic finale he pulled out of his pocket the ball he had won from me and held it on high.

Imagine the scene. Behind him were the silver cups and shields he had won because of a year's successful selling; in his pocket were the air tickets and the cheques. And there he stood as happy as a boy with his first bicycle, bragging about winning a golf ball worth a few pence.

This is the Killer Instinct. The prizes he had won were history; they were part of the year that was past. The ball was today, it was *now*. Tomorrow he would need a new dragon to slay, a new mountain to climb, a new maiden to rescue. The Killer Instinct grows with what it feeds on; it is an addiction, and those afflicted with it need their regular fix or life becomes tasteless and dreary.

I once gave a series of talks to groups of motor-car sales people around the country. It was restricted to the top men in their teams, so these were at the upper end of the spectrum in their industry, running all the way from good through very good to great. It was an exhilarating experience for me because I was working with people who were successful, not only because of their expertise in selling but because of their attitudes towards their jobs.

Anyway, I became more involved with these men than I usually do with sales groups, to the extent that we had several bull sessions after working hours. As with most salesmen it didn't need more than a few drinks to start them talking –

talking as in 'swanking'. I noticed an interesting thing when they talked about the sales they had made; the *good* salesmen talked about the *big* deals they had pulled off, where they had sold five units here and ten units there. They were obviously interested in the *size* of the order.

The élite among them? They talked about the *tough* sales they had made, the ones where even if it was only one unit, they had fought off the combined weight of three strong competitors. The Killer Instinct again.

I was introduced to a man who, I was told proudly, had won a regional amateur tennis tournament and who was fancied for a national title. When we had been talking for a while I said lightly that if I ever had to face him across a net he would have to stand on one leg to make the match more even. Well, I said it merely for something to say, but he took it more seriously than I had intended – perhaps he was one of those people who take most things seriously – and he said: 'No, if we ever played each other I would have to do everything I could to beat you as decisively as I could. I can't afford to play a friendly game of tennis.'

I can't afford to play a friendly game. He meant, I suppose, that once he began taking it the slightest bit easy he would be in danger of losing the fine cutting edge, the compulsion to win – the Killer Instinct.

Here's an example which proves, more conclusively than anything I can think of, that the size of the kill has nothing to do with the feeling of achievement, that it is the excitement of the chase that gives the winner his personal high. I was out with a sales supervisor on a call to an industrial customer where the discussion centred on the purchase of several large stationary power units. The potential order was enormous – each of these monsters cost more than a Jaguar – and I sat fascinated as the sales supervisor used every weapon in his sales armoury to get the signature on the order, which he finally did.

As we walked through the factory on our way out I was congratulating him on the successful sale. Suddenly he stopped and I saw that he was examining a can of oil which stood next to a crankshaft grinder. He spoke briefly to the machine-minder and said to me: 'These guys are using a terrible cutting oil on this grinder. I'm going back to the buyer and sell him a couple of cans of good stuff.'

I said: 'Have you lost your mind? You have just tied up an order which has made your quota for three months. Right now that buyer is sitting wondering if he did the right thing in signing your order. You know this; it's the natural reaction to making any big buying decision. He'll get over it and realise that he has done exactly what he should have done, but in the meantime he is in a post-decision anxiety state. And you want to show your face in that office for the sale of two lousy cans of oil?'

I admit I didn't go back with him; my moral courage has its limits. I waited in the car for him, and I shall never forget his look of triumph as he slid into the seat next to me and threw into my lap the order for two cans of cutting oil, value under ten pounds.

I am giving many examples of the Killer Instinct simply because it is a lot easier to do this than it is to explain exactly what it is. It has to do with dedication but it is a lot more than simple dedication. There is single-mindedness of purpose but it goes further than that. Those who are blessed or afflicted (choose your own term) with it seem to channel all their efforts and energies into it, setting aside everything else, and I mean *everything*. They are often not the most comfortable people to work with, play with or live with; marriages, families and homes have been broken up because of the need to win, the hatred of losing.

Let's go a little deeper into this point, it's important. We have been examining the exploits and successes of the winner, but let us recognise right here and now that some of his characteristics, and the Killer Instinct is one of them, do not make for the easiest of bedfellows. Don't get the idea from anything here that being a winner is necessarily a cosy situation to be in. It isn't. It's much more comfortable in the rut with the rest of the mob.

At about this stage it's likely that an old saw has entered your mind. You could be saying to yourself: 'Yes, he's making the point that "Nice guys don't win".'

By no means, and I don't believe the saying anyway. Nice guys often do win; of course they do. I have made a lifelong study of the winner, and if none of them were decent human beings I wouldn't have bothered to spend my time on them. But what do we mean by 'Nice guys', anyway? Who are these people?

Well, there goes one now. He is chairman of the local tuberculosis association, does his stint fund-raising for Guide Dogs for the Blind, would give you the shirt off his back, hasn't an enemy in the world and has a smile and a friendly word for everyone. He has the unshakeable conviction that his future is in the restaurant business, and his long-suffering father has staked him to four separate and distinct ventures in this field; he has managed to go broke in all four of them. A nice guy but hardly a winner, and his record seems to indicate that nice guys don't win.

But think of the good ones who do win. Think of the many, many wonderful people who have won and are winning in every business, sport, political, religious and social sphere. They have the Killer Instinct but that doesn't make them sociopaths or misanthropes. In fact it is often the losers who turn against their fellow man in a spasm of hate for the circumstance which has brought them down. The Killer Instinct has nothing to do with the ethics or morals of anyone who has it; Joan of Arc and Cesare Borgia, Churchill and Hitler all had it. It shows in the words and actions of heroes and villains, saints and sinners.

I want it! How do I get it?

I'm not sure that I can tell you how to acquire the Killer Instinct if you don't have it now. I have a feeling that there could be a slight Catch-22 situation here, in that you may have to have it before you can get it. Let's see.

There was a young politician who was such a keen and tireless worker for his party that it was clear that sooner or later he would have to be offered the chance of a seat in parliament. The chance came, but it was no birthday present. A by-election turned up in a constituency which had been a stronghold of the opposing party for many years. The young man's seniors decided to contest the seat as a matter of policy, of showing the flag, not with any idea of actually winning, and they threw our hero into the arena, feeling that it would do a good job of blooding him. He knew the score, and entered the campaign with less than his usual enthusiasm.

Well, he didn't win. Nobody expected him to win. What he did do though was give the opposing candidate the shock of his life. He had expected a landslide in his favour and it turned out to be a real nail-biter of a finish. Our man had, as the campaign progressed, become caught up in the excitement of the battle, and his enthusiasm had communicated itself to the voters who had turned out in their thousands and very nearly caused a major upset. He did so well that the warlords of the party machine promised him a much better chance in the next election; a safer seat, in fact.

What was this neo-Disraeli's reaction? 'No bloody fear!' He said. 'Gimme a tough one – something I can get my teeth into!'

He had acquired the Killer Instinct and he had got it by *doing*. Would he have got it if the result of the election had been the easy win for the opposition that everyone had expected? Who knows? Maybe not.

Poor boy or rich boy?

So now we examine an intriguing problem. Does the Killer Instinct come because of something which was denied a person? Do people from deprived backgrounds acquire it because they have to fight to gain their place in the sun which has come easily to the silver-spoon-in-the-mouth people?

Evidence is contradictory. A survey was done of young people going to university, with half of those involved coming from well-to-do families and half from the wrong side of the street. Now, every gutter-to-glory tale tells us that the poor boy is the one with the motivation, right? He is imbued with the desire to gain for himself those things his pa never had. The scion of the rich family has no such urge; he has had things easy all his life so far, so why should he slog away now?

The survey, to the surprise of the people running it, showed no significant difference between the two groups; the poor boys didn't do any better than the rich boys. In fact there was a very slight reading the other way; the rich ones did fractionally better, although not enough to be statistically significant.

Which leads us down another interesting path. There is a school of thought which believes that there may be a sound, logical reason for hiring job applicants on the 'old school tie' basis, that much-derided practice of former days. The theory is that the boy from the expensive (and therefore more exclusive) school comes from a background of winners. His family and friends are accustomed to the trappings of success, and he therefore carries with him the confidence – or arrogance, if you like – of success.

I really don't know. Make your own decision.

But to get back to the Killer Instinct. Gary Player is one of the most competitive golfers in the world. He brings to the game a dedication and will to win unrivalled by anyone except perhaps the legendary Ben Hogan. Jack Nicklaus once said of his friend: 'If Gary was five inches taller and weighted forty pounds more he would be the greatest golfer of all time.' Or words to that effect.

Now with respect to Mr Nicklaus (who in fact *is* the greatest golfer of all time) he misses the point. Isn't it the fact that Player *was* smaller and lighter than the other professionals which made him as determined as he is? Who knows. Certainly, he brings a tremendous enthusiasm to everything he does. Ask him the way to the post office and he will take you there, talking all the way about how the postal service could be improved.

Another example, and this also seems to support the theory of the deprived youngster fighting his way to the top. A boy failed the high-school examination which would have allowed him to enter university, something which he very much wanted to do. He was intelligent and industrious, and the reason for his failure was the fact that his schoolteacher had recommended to his parents that he take a group of subjects in which he had little aptitude and no interest.

He battled through his early life in business, fighting his way up the ladder in competition with other young men who had university degrees. His was a true success story; he ended up running a large industrial company.

Forty years later, almost to the day when he sat in the school hall to write and fail his matriculation, that boy, now a man at the summit of his success, went back to that school. It was late afternoon and everyone had gone home. He parked his car and entered the school buildings where he found the janitor. He explained that he was an Old Boy and asked if he could look around. The janitor, impressed by the expensive suit, the luxury car and the large tip he was given, readily gave his permission. Would sir like to be shown anything in particular? No, sir would like to walk around on his own. Sir was welcome.

He walked into his old classroom, looked out of the windows at the playing-fields, looked in at the library, the debating chamber, the gymnasium. At last he came to the hall where he had written the hated examinations. His steps echoed in the vast, empty auditorium. He stood in the centre of the bare floor and looked up at the platform where the teachers would sit at assembly. He said: 'Go to hell.' He said it louder: 'Go to hell!' He shouted it: 'GO TO HELL!' Then he walked out, nodded at the wide-eyed janitor, got into his car and drove away.

Forty years it took him to gain the right to go into that hall and stand and yell his defiance and contempt at the ghosts of those long-dead teachers. Forty years, and he never forgot. Perhaps, had he taken the right subjects, passed the exams and gone to university he might never have reached the high pinnacle of success which he did achieve. We shall never know. We do know what gave him the Killer Instinct – the all-consuming need to *show* them, which stayed with him all his life.

There is something about that story you don't like? You find it vindictive? Hellfire, I'm not asking you to *approve* of him, I'm simply saying, that's the Killer Instinct at work. But in any case you needn't have the picture of a man whose whole life was soured by the corrosion in his soul put there by the action of an unthinking schoolteacher. I assure you that this man enjoys his life to the full; he is a wonderful husband and father and a hell of a guy at a party. He just happens to be a winner, and one of the things about him which makes him a winner is his Killer Instinct.

Must I have it to be a winner?

I don't say that you can't be a winner without the Killer Instinct. We all know people whose talents are so great that they manage to coast through life with nothing driving them; but remember, those are the superpeople. In these pages we can spare a passing glance at Steffi Graf, Margaret Thatcher, David Hockney, Wilbur Smith, Lee Iacocca and others like them. We can even use them to make one point or another, but we are not going to set them up as examples to copy. They are the superpeople, and the whole theme of this book is *that it doesn't take a superman*. None of those people need to read this. With the characteristics they bring to the business of living, for them to study how to be successful would be like a fish taking swimming lessons. Ordinary people like us have to work at it.

None of which means that the great ones don't work at what they do, nor does it mean that they always do it well. That writer tears up whole chapters in disgust, that football star falls over his own feet, that politician makes an ill-considered remark which not even the greenest tyro would

---

Only mediocrity is always at its best.

Max Beerbohm

---

make, this big business magnate decides to buy a company which loses his group millions. They make the mistakes all right, but when they do they have the knowledge to correct the mistakes, almost automatically. We have to try a little harder.

Which is good news. The habit of trying a little harder is not a difficult one to acquire, and it truly is a habit, and nothing is easier to perpetuate than a habit. Once we have the habit of trying a little harder it is like any other habit; it is easier to keep on doing it than it is to stop it.

And don't forget that the term is *try* a little harder, not *work* harder. The Killer Instinct doesn't mean suicide from overwork.

Come on, come on; how do I get it?

Well, you may have it thrust on you because of one incident in your life. I met a man on a flight who told me how it came to him. His wife had warned him that a couple of his business shirts were showing signs of wear and had told him to get some more. He went into the store where he always bought his shirts, and he was served by the assistant who had known him for years. 'Shirts? You bet,' the assistant said, and reached behind him. Then he stopped and said, 'No, of course – these are too expensive for you,' and he walked away to where the cheaper shirts were displayed.

'That one remark did it,' the man said. 'I realised that all my life I had been putting up with second-best. Not only that, but the people who knew me – family, friends, colleagues at work, even shop-assistants, damn it – they all *expected* me to be satisfied with the second-rate, the not-quite-so-good, the economy class, the off-the-peg.'

He stood in that shop and in that instant he acquired the Killer Instinct. He called to the assistant who was pulling the house-brand shirts from the shelf. 'Hey – come back here!' he said. 'Give me three of these.' He walked out of the store with his top-of-the-line shirts and straight into a jeweller across the road, where he bought his wife a good-looking eternity ring. She squealed with delight at the present but then looked worried. 'But darling, can we afford it?'

He said: 'From *today* we can.'

He was lucky. A thoughtless and tactless remark changed his life. Those of us who are not fortunate to be hit by a similar lightning bolt have to acquire the Killer Instinct in other ways. How?

Well, first let's recognise that the term itself is misleading. I hereby confess that I used it to shock you into realising that the winner has something – a fire in the belly, perhaps – which the man in the mob doesn't have. It doesn't mean that you walk around with a flick-knife and your gun slung low, zapping everyone who thwarts you or gets in your way. The Killer Instinct doesn't have anything to do with anyone else at all, in fact. It is an attitude which is very much *I* and not *you other people*. It says: 'I am going to succeed in this no matter what other people say or think about me. This has nothing to do with anyone else. This is a straight fight between me and Life, and I am going to win.'

You might read that last bit again and ask yourself: does it express what you would like to feel? Read it again. Absorb it into your thinking. Feel it. Feel the truth of it. It *is* true, isn't it? Believe it. Never let it go.

4
THE SUCCESS, THE FAILURE, AND THE NON-SUCCESS

We tend to label people as either successes or failures, but of course this is too much of a yes/no, right/wrong, go/no go distinction. Between the success and the failure lies a person who doesn't fit into either of these slots.

He is the Non-success.

The best way to describe the Non-success is to look at all three characters. What follows are actual examples, changed only as much as is needed to avoid identification.

Horace is a doctor in general practice. He is in his mid-forties, happily married with two children. He has a Hobiecat which he sails with fair skill and tremendous enthusiasm. His practice is in a new housing estate which suits Horace perfectly as this means lots of newly-married couples, and young marrieds means that there are lots of babies around, and Horace loves babies. His greatest joy is seeing women through fat ankles, morning sickness and back pain, to the big moment when he and they work as a team to launch a new and noisy statistic into an already overpopulated world. After nearly twenty years he still manages to get excited about fixing three-month colic and projectile vomiting. He is adored by his patients, respected by his medical confrères and cherished by his friends. One has no difficulty in describing Horace as a success.

Cecil was a salesman in a pest-control company. He did well enough to be promoted to area supervisor and eventually to regional manager. One day it dawned on him that the pest-control business was labour-intensive rather than capital-intensive, which simply means that in order to set up in business for oneself it isn't necessary to have a million in the bank. The sprayers and pesticides didn't cost much, and all that was needed was a second-hand van and two semi-skilled assistants to start a new pest-control company.

So Cecil went into business for himself. He was able to persuade many of the customers of his old company to move over to him. He concentrated on giving high-quality personal service to every customer, and his business soon prospered; his bright yellow vans ('Be certain with Cecil') were a familiar sight in the district. Soon he was so busy directing his team from his office suite that he was no longer able to give customers the personal service which had drawn them to him at the start of his venture, but his sales figures were impressive and they increased every year.

Then a big national pest-control outfit moved into the district. They took a look at the competition and decided that Cecil would be a nuisance to them, so they approached him with a take-over offer. Cecil laughed them out of his office. 'Try to take over this territory and I'll blow you guys out of the water,' he said. He had lots of fun describing the interview to his wife and friends. 'The nerve of those guys! Let them come – I love a good fight.'

The big company worked on a very simple creed: If you can't join 'em, beat 'em. They hit the district with heavy promotions, special deals, and prices below Cecil's *costs*. They didn't bother to blow Cecil out of the water; they simply sat back out of range and watched him sink. It took eight months. One bright and sunny morning, after urgent calls from his bank manager and his auditor, Cecil wrote a note to his wife and walked out of his ninth-floor office by way of the window. We can agree that Cecil had been a failure.

Eddie was always in the top ten at school and his special aptitude for figures more or less dictated that he would be an accountant. He had no trouble piling up all the required letters behind his name at university and his *Magna cum Laude* ensured that he was quickly offered a job with an international firm, a market leader in the rigid plastics field. His career path was mapped out for him when his superiors realised that he was a bright boy who toed the line at all times, was safely married to a suitable woman, and was in every way a good corporation man. Eddie is now forty years old. His house is immaculate, his yearly holidays to the mountains or the sea are enjoyable, he has a good pension plan going for him, he is healthy.

His wife arranged a party for his fortieth birthday; just a few friends around for dinner. When the guests had left, Eddie's wife came through to the living-room to find Eddie with a last drink in his hand, staring into space. To her question, was anything wrong, Eddie blinked, smiled, kissed her and thanked her for the party. They went upstairs with their arms around each other.

Now, Eddie looks like a success, doesn't he? From every point of view he seems to have it made. Yet he is not a success, although no one in the whole wide world knows it but Eddie. The thing is that his high marks at school obscured another talent – he was the delight and joy of his art teacher. His delicate water-colours and his authoritative charcoal sketches were of a standard higher than she had ever seen in a boy of any age.

Eddie's parents were from solid and respectable and traditional backgrounds, and while it pleased them that Eddie was able to bring home such pretty drawings and paintings, it never occurred to them to think of this talent as anything but a hobby, a pastime, something to do over the weekend while during the week Eddie got on with the serious business of accountancy. At a PTA meeting his art teacher raised the subject with Eddie's people; she said that it was likely that with encouragement and the right training Eddie could be a leading artist. Did his mother, for one moment, have a wistful look in her eye? His father's eye showed nothing but barely concealed impatience; his son was not going to spend his life in a grubby garret, drinking cheap wine and consorting with people of limited talent and questionable morals. He didn't come out and say all that but his manner was indication enough that the art teacher was talking rubbish. Eddie was a dutiful son and after the failure of the art teacher's approach he went along with his father's wishes.

Eddie has had strong hints from management that he is in line for a directorship. He is naturally pleased that his future with the company is assured, and he has already started looking for a new house; he has already bought his wife a diamond pendant for their fifteenth wedding anniversary.

Eddie's parents are still alive and they see Eddie regularly. They are also pleased that he has done so well in business. The only thing which his mother can't understand is that Eddie, with all the talent which he showed for drawing and painting at school, has not so much as picked up a brush since he went into business. She once asked him why, and his brusque: 'I've no time for that sort of thing,' was not like him at all.

Now, Eddie can by no means be described as a failure. By all reasonable criteria he is a success. But we know better, don't we? Eddie is a Non-success, and the tragedy of our time is that the world is full of them.

The Non-success goes through life with the feeling that somewhere along the line he has been screwed. This feeling can be anything from a mild, occasional, nagging irritation, all the way to a much deeper and more intense condition which can lead to a complete emotional breakdown. Material gain has nothing to do with being a Non-success; there are wealthy Non-successes as well as pauper ones.

Now is the time for you to do something which you must not duck. If you don't do this then don't bother to turn the page. Any further reading will be a waste of time for you. You have to ask yourself a question. It is a tough question. What makes it tough is that you have to take a good long, hard look at yourself, which is always one of the most difficult things we can do, which is why we duck it. Here is the question, and don't duck it!

Am I a Non-success?

Well, are you? Not an easy question to put to yourself, is it – let alone to answer. I am going to put down some secondary questions which may help you to answer the big one, but first I have an admission to make.

This book was written for one person only. I wrote it for the Non-success. It isn't for the success; he doesn't need it. It isn't for the failure; it won't help him. Only the Non-success has any chance of getting anything from it. Now, I should have put on the cover of the book FOR THE USE OF THE NON-SUCCESS ONLY. I didn't because then you would have rejected it, wouldn't you? You would have said: 'That's for failures, and I am not a failure.' You would have been deeply offended if anyone had offered the book for you to read.

But now we know what a Non-success is. We know that he is not a failure. If the questions below indicate that you are a Non-success then you know that you needn't feel depressed or offended or suicidal. *Non-success is not failure.* The Non-success is not a loser, although he is a long way from being a winner. That is our job here, to turn him into one.

All right, look in your mirror:

1. Do I find myself glancing through the Jobs Offered section in the classifieds, even though I have no idea of changing jobs?

2. Do I ever visualise myself in another life-style? Do I see myself as a farmer, a writer, a pilot, an architect?

3. Do I sometimes question people about the jobs they do, in much greater depth than mere politeness?

4. At the end of my leave period do I get a sinking feeling about going back to a year of the same work which is much more than simple regret at the end of the holidays?

5. Have I ever had the notion of selling everything up and getting away from it all? While everyone thinks of this at one time or another, has it become a fairly frequent and familiar thought in the back of my mind?

'Yes' to any of them? You could be a Non-success. Of course, there is nothing scientific about that little quiz, and now that you have answered it only you know the depth or intensity to which your 'yes' answers went. But if any of the questions seemed to hit a nerve somewhere then you could indeed qualify to join the ranks of the Non-successes.

I was you!

I was a Non-success for so long that if I thought about it at all I must have decided that it was to be my life's work. Let me tell you about it.

After faffing around for a few years with no real sense of

direction I drifted into selling. Lots of people do, simply because it is one of the easiest jobs to get into; you don't need a degree or an apprenticeship or any qualifications whatever. Once I realised that in order to become a good salesman it was necessary to forget almost everything that had been taught to me by sales trainers, I became fairly good and did quite well – so well in fact that they eventually made me a sales manager. I was now on the ladder which would lead me ineluctably up to a senior executive job, and although I had no way of knowing it, I was becoming firmly entrenched as a Non-success.

It's an insidious thing, this business of becoming a Non-success. You don't have the faintest idea of what is happening until you wake up one morning and bingo, you're it. It hit me one day when I had taken an afternoon off to play golf. As it happened the weather turned bad on us with the wind carrying a nasty drizzle which started when we were well out on the course. I cursed our luck in picking a bad day for the game, and my partner said: 'Don't cry, buddy; it still beats working!' 'You bet,' I agreed. 'It beats working.'

Afterwards, thinking about it on my way home, I was appalled. Did I really mean it? Did sloshing my way around a wet course, having to wipe my glasses before each shot and on top of all that, not hitting the ball well that day – did that beat doing the work that I did every day of my life? If it did then something was very wrong indeed.

The terrible problem is that one gets locked into the Non-success syndrome so very easily. Slowly, link by link, we ourselves forge the chains which bind us until before we realise it we are imprisoned. For one thing, I was tied into a certain income bracket. I had a large mortgage, my daughters went to expensive schools, we sat in the best seats at the opera, we dined out regularly and three cars stood in our drive. I was reminded of the actor who said that it had taken him twenty years to realise that he had no talent for acting, but by then he couldn't stop because he was already famous and making too much money. It was no joke to me.

My personal fairy godmother came in the unlikely guise of an advertising space salesman who called on me at work. When we had done our business and were relaxing over a cup of coffee he got me talking about my own triumphs and disasters. He was easy to talk to and I may have opened up more than I usually do to strangers. Before he left he made the remark which helped me to change my life. He said: 'Mr Beer, forgive me for being intrusive, but I don't understand why you are working for other people. What I have learnt about you in the last twenty minutes convinces me that you should be working for yourself.'

What does he know, I thought, and that evening I related the incident to my wife to show her what sort of oddballs I had to deal with every day. To my surprise she didn't laugh. Instead she said: 'Well?'

'Well what?' I said.

'Well, what about it? You're not happy in your job. Why not go out on your own?'

I was flabbergasted. 'What do you mean, I'm not happy? Have I ever said I'm not happy? Of course I'm happy!'

She said: 'Remember me? I'm your wife. I *know* you. You are not happy in your job.'

So between them my wife and a space salesman knocked me out of the comfortable rut of the Non-success. I started Michael Beer Training Clinics, which was a rather pretentious name for me, with an underpaid secretary and some second-hand office furniture. No capital, no clients; just the idea that I had been a Non-success long enough.

Was I a success? Yes, from the very first day. Of course, it was three months before I got my first client; I had to sell two of my cars; I had several dramatic interviews with my bank manager; they threatened to repossess my typewriter.

But I was a success. I woke every morning eagerly looking forward to the challenge ahead. Make fifty calls this week and get fifty turn-downs. Great! That's fifty nearer to my first clinic. I was doing what I wanted to do, and I was a success. I learnt that hamburger and cheap wine as a success tasted

> Knowledge of what is possible is the beginning of happiness.
>
> *George Santayana*

better than Châteaubriand and Cabernet Sauvignon as a Non-success.

This is not an account of my career path. The story of Michael Beer is of intense interest only to Michael Beer. Also, I hope that what I did will not be taken by everybody who reads this to mean that they should immediately resign their jobs and go out on their own. Indeed, the reverse is often true, where someone who is working on his own and hating it could leave the world of the Non-success and by joining the right company could become the success he deserves to be.

In fact there may be no reason to change your job. You may be a Non-success at the moment, but who says you have to change what you are doing? Perhaps the answer is not to change what you are doing but how you are doing it. Make sense? Let's see.

5
SELF-RENEWAL

. . . Or, 'Knock me down and I'll flatten you as I bounce back.'

Let's look at the interesting business of the odds in gambling. A roulette wheel has thirty-six numbers and a zero. That zero is the reason that the bank *always* wins and that over any extended period of time the gambler *always* loses, and no 'foolproof' system ever devised can change this. The zero, of course, is not a number; it is not odd or even; it is not red or black. So if you bet on any of these and the zero turns up, you lose.

Interesting, but what has any of that to do with Self-renewal, and just what is Self-renewal, anyway?

Self-renewal is the capacity of resilience. It is the ability to bounce back in the face of rebuffs, disappointments, scorn, prejudice and derision. It is an odd mixture of perseverance, persistence, assurance, conviction, and plain damned pig-headedness.

Where is courage in that list? Doesn't courage form a part of Self-renewal? I don't think it does, but I could be wrong, so let's talk about it.

I have a theory about courage. It may not be original; it's quite likely that someone else thought it up years ago. I believe that, unlike other human characteristics, at which we become

[51]

more and more skilled the more we practise or use them, with courage the opposite applies. We are each born with this little box of courage inside us. Every time we find a need for courage we reach into the little box and take some out and use it. *We use it up.* What is left in the box does not grow; interest is not added to it; it does not mature or become stronger or better.

Then one day we reach into the box for another piece of courage. The box is empty; the courage has all been used up.

This is a phenomenon well known in time of war. Those incredibly brave people who, again and again, parachuted behind enemy lines to work with the resistance forces; the soldiers who, time after time, threw themselves against superior numbers; the bomber crews who every day set off on raids on well-protected targets – in many cases for these people the time came when they woke one morning and reached into their boxes and found them empty. They couldn't do it any more.

You see these people with their empty boxes and it is one of the most pitiful sights you can ever experience. Walk in the public parks, and when one of the bundles of dirty rags approaches you, instead of thrusting a coin at him and turning away, look into his eyes. *Really* look; hold his eyes with yours. If he is not completely stoned with hooch or meths or pot you will see in those eyes something worse than terror, worse than agony; you will see despair, the complete negation of hope.

I have seen this look in the eyes of men I have had to turn down for jobs, and you don't have to be involved in mankind to feel sick about it. There is always a little of the 'There but for the grace of God go I' guilt about seeing a fellow human being in that situation.

– Which is why we need Self-renewal, because no one knows when his box of courage will be empty, and when you run out of it you had better have a damned good substitute.

Self-renewal is that substitute.

One way to make Self-renewal work for you is one which is well known to rehabilitated alcoholics and drug-users, those admirable people who have dragged themselves out of the morass of dependence on their particular demons and are leading normal, useful lives. As most people know, the members of AA never say: 'I was an alcoholic.' The fact that they may not have had a drink for ten years has nothing to do with it; the monkey is always there and ready to climb on to their backs again. They will tell you (and have you noticed the faint gleam of pride there): 'I *am* an alcoholic.' It is something they live with, every hour of every day.

How do they manage, these wonderful people? They do it *one day at a time*. The idea of fighting their problem for the rest of their lives would be too much for anyone to handle, so they don't try to handle it. Every day they say to themselves: 'I can handle this for twenty-four hours. No need to look further than that; just for this day I can beat it.'

Renewing yourself for the rest of your life? That could be tough. Just for one day? That you can handle.

You are not an alcoholic. But this works for thousands and thousands of winners in all walks of life, in every circumstance. I recently talked to a woman who has started her own business – it doesn't matter what, because I don't want to identify her. She is having a tough time because of the age-old problem of small, new ventures; she is running out of ready cash to pay the rent of her premises, buy supplies, meet the payroll of her small staff and generally have money at hand for the day-to-day expenses which always crop up. Work is coming in nicely, but the gap between income and outgo is still – well, it's just that; a gap.

How is she handling it? One day at a time. She said: 'I wake every morning and I say to myself: right, here's another day. Now, the world is not coming to an end today; nobody is going to close me down in the next twenty-four hours. The bank has turned down my request for a further loan but at least my present overdraft facilities have been extended for another month. I don't have to meet my payroll for four days. There are no bills so urgent that the roof will fall in if I don't pay them this week. I have three pieces of work in progress and a good chance of two more coming in. I can *handle* today.'

The corrosion of worry

One thing which can stop Self-renewal in its tracks is the corrosive effect of plain, ordinary worry. The idiotic thing about worry is that everyone knows what a futile exercise it is, but that doesn't stop us doing it. Naturally we should be careful what we are talking about here. We must distinguish between *concern* which is logical, positive and essential, and *worry* which is illogical, negative and useless. The knowledge of the uselessness of worrying doesn't seem to help us to stop it. Why not? Well, perhaps we feel that we *should* worry. We can feel guilty if we don't worry – we are in this bind, we have these problems – perhaps the gods will be angry if we don't worry!

Concerned? Yes, of course we should be concerned. You are a professional football-player and it seems that you are losing the fine control of the ball which made you famous. Your factory is committed to making oscillating paravanes and the swing seems to be to reciprocating paravanes. Your power in the upper register has made you one of the world's best operatic sopranos, but you have just been rejected for the role of Mimi in *La Bohème* in favour of a relative unknown. You and your spouse decided that you could just afford to buy that house at 13 per cent interest on the bond, especially since you were due for an increase in salary, so you went ahead and signed. Now the interest has gone up to 14½ and the increase in salary was not as much as you expected.

Now, all of these situations should cause concern. There

has been an unwelcome change which calls for action of some sort. What the action will be will depend on what you have decided after careful thought and planning – but you can't do any careful thought and planning if you are worrying, because worrying is a full-time occupation. Worry is like the parasite living in the body of the host animal. The animal goes about its business apparently unaffected by the parasite, but it gradually gets weaker as the parasite takes its power little by little, until at last it becomes unable to catch its food and it dies. Worry is like that. We can go about our business apparently unaffected, but the worry is there, weakening our resolve, inhibiting our actions, until *the worry itself* becomes the major problem, until we are literally unable to handle the problem which caused the worry in the first place.

This produces something which we could call, not a vicious circle, but a descending spiral. The problem causes worry, the worry reduces our ability to handle the problem effectively, this exacerbates the problem, which causes more worry – and away we go, round and round and down and down, sucked into the maelstrom of despair.

Self-renewal! Without it we will surely lose.

Which brings us back to the roulette wheel we first talked about. One marvellous way to create Self-renewal in ourselves is simply to trust the law of averages. This is a fascinating law because in logic it actually doesn't exist. Take the roulette wheel. It has no memory; each time it is spun it is a brand-new game, as though it had never spun before. Therefore the fact that the number 19 has come up three times in a row is no reason for it not to come up again on the fourth spin. In a thousand spins of the wheel there is therefore no reason why it should not come up one thousand times – but of course *it never does*. There are thirty-six numbers on the wheel – thirty-six numbers and the zero. With a perfectly balanced wheel we know that the number 19 will, in a thousand spins, come up just about one thousand divided by thirty-seven, or about twenty-seven times. This is an elementary illustration of the law of averages.

What has this to do with Self-renewal? Well, let's take the case of a salesman to whom I owe more than I can ever repay. I met him only once for less than twenty minutes, I don't recall his name, I would pass him in the street without recognising him – but he taught me a lesson which has benefited me immeasurably. This is what happened.

I saw an advertisement in a trade magazine for an office dictating machine and it seemed to me that this was what I had been looking for. I called the company and asked them to send a salesman around with a demonstration model. He came and started demonstrating the machine, but he hadn't got far when I stopped him. 'Hang on,' I said. 'Doesn't this thing have a speaker facility? Can you use it only with the ear-phones?'

He said, 'That's right. That's the way the typists like to use it.'

I said: 'I'm sorry. I must have misunderstood your advertisement. I have to have the choice of speaker and headphones. I can't buy your machine.' We discussed it for a moment and he agreed that for my needs his machine wouldn't do the job. I said: 'I want to apologise. I've wasted your time, getting you to come out here, and I'm a salesman too, and I hate people wasting my time. Sorry.'

He was packing up his demonstration kit. He said: 'Please don't apologise, Mr Beer. In fact, I have to thank you for a £200 order.'

I said: 'I didn't make myself clear. I'm not buying your product.'

He said: 'I know you're not. All the same, thank you for the £200 order.'

I said: 'Will you develop that theme for me? How am I giving you an order without buying anything?'

He smiled. 'Mr Beer, I have a demonstration-to-sales ratio of four to one. Every 400 times I demonstrate this machine I get 100 sales. The machine costs £800. Thank you for the £200 order.'

Well! Do you see how this man's mind works? He didn't hear me say 'No.' He never hears *anybody* say 'No.' Every time he shows his product to someone he is one-quarter of the way to the next order. Would you say that he has Self-renewal? You bet he has – he has a job where nobody ever turns him down, where he gets no rebuffs, no refusals, where he never has a failure.

Of course, in order for this idea to work for him he must keep his demonstrating skills sharp, he must make sure that he is calling on the right people, he must keep an eye on what the opposition is doing – he must, in a word, do his best on every call. He can't amble through his working day half-asleep and expect that he will still get his four-to-one ratio. But so long as he stays on top of his job the ratio will work for him.

– And all that is simply an example of the law of averages at work.

To go back to our roulette-wheel analogy. Everyone knows that the owners of the casinos don't go broke. The gamblers often do, but never the casinos. Why? The law of averages. We tend to say that the people at Las Vegas or Monte Carlo must make trillions, but how do they make it? *On the zero.* Consider it; put a bet on the red or the black and win, and you double your money. Odd or even, over eighteen or under eighteen, you double your money. But that is a fifty-fifty chance, and the casino doesn't get rich that way. But when the zero comes up the bank scoops the pool – and it comes up twenty-seven times in every thousand spins. Let the ball drop into the green slot of the zero and everyone loses (except the ones who have bet on the zero itself). So you know what the casino makes; it makes one-thirty-seventh of the total money bet, *and it makes it on every spin of the wheel*, whether it pays out or not.

There is of course another sneaky way in which it wins;

there are thirty-seven slots for the ball to fall into, but they pay out only thirty-five to one. Incidentally, if you play a wheel with *two* zeros, why not save yourself the trouble and simply throw your money out of the window?

Now, we have taken some time over this analogy but it has been worth-while to drive the point home that the simplest way to gain Self-renewal is to believe in the law of averages. It *does* work. Flip a coin five times and see it come down heads every time. Flip it one more time and you know that there is no logical reason for it not to come down heads again; the coin has no memory. But you know that if you flip it one thousand times it will come down heads almost exactly 500 of those times – *always*.

So; the winner doesn't lie back, tip his hat over his eyes and wait for the law of averages to work for him. He gives it everything he's got, never letting off for an instant. But he knows that if he keeps going as well as he possibly can, the law of averages will work for him – *always*.

That's what Self-renewal is all about.

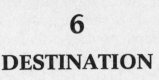

6

DESTINATION

. . . Or, 'I know where I'm going, so stand aside or I'll walk right over you to get there.'

One of the winner's consistent characteristics is a powerful, all-consuming sense of Destination; *he knows where he is going*. He knows where he wants to go, he sees the road he is going to take to get there, and in most cases he has a very good idea of how long the trip will take him.

This is a must for the winner. Without it there is little chance of winning.

Unless you know where you are going, how will you know what course to chart? How will you know which way to go? How will you know when you've got there? Yet if you have a sense of destination you are already half-way along the track, while the mob is still standing around at the starting-gate.

I deliberately don't use the word 'Destiny' as the heading for this chapter because I don't want to make this section sound in any way mystical or overly profound. It is true that throughout history people have had a sense of destiny which has driven them to achieve wonderful things, and one can't imagine Boadicea or Moses or Bolívar being content with merely a destination. But do remember that here we are not dealing with the immortals. We are discussing you, not some superbeing. Ordinary people, not Luther or Garibaldi.

The wonderful thing about a sense of destination is that by itself, with nothing else at all, it gives you such a tremendous advantage over the mob. I have said before that most people don't really know where they're going. Oh, they know that if nothing terrible happens they will probably be workshop manager in about ten years, that by that time Aunt Ethel will have died and the old house will be theirs, that they should start thinking about having another child if they are going to have one, and some time they would probably take the trip to South America they have always talked about. But that is hardly a sense of destination, that is merely a list of stations that the train stops at along the way. Those people don't know where they are going because they have never thought about it. Now, along comes someone who *has* thought about it and what happens? He shoots past the thousands whose lives are in neutral. It happens every time.

The ones without a sense of destination stand in awe of those who have it, and this by itself gives the winner the inside track.

Not right away, of course; show that you have a strong sense of where you are going and you will encounter first bewilderment and then often derision, and verbal and even physical opposition. You are rocking the boat, you see. It's cosy here, drifting along with the rest of the mob, so who does he think he is, making waves? And waves aren't all he's making, either; he's making us all look silly. Chuck a brick at him. But eventually when the mob sees that your destination is clear and that you are well on your way to reaching it, then by golly do you often get a turnaround of attitude! That's when you get the hangers-on who want a free ride with you, the distant acquaintances who are suddenly your old and close friends and who would like a bit of the goodies you have managed to gather on your way to your destination. They have no destination of their own but they are more than happy to use yours now that you have found it.

Now, because nothing ever happens neatly (look around

you and you will discover, if you haven't already done so, what an untidy world we inhabit), this sense of destination doesn't come at a set time for us. Boys don't get it automatically when their voices break, girls don't get it automatically when their chests become interesting. Sometimes it comes quite late in life. Raymond Chandler, the famous detective-story writer, was a business executive when he picked up a thriller to read on a business trip, as so many of us have done. Having read it he said, as so many of us have done, 'Hell, I could write that stuff.' So many of us have done it and, having said it, have turned away from it. Chandler was the exception; he saw his destination in life and reached for it. He grabbed hold of it and made it his own – but the point of this story is that his first book was not published until he was fifty-one years old. Your destination can appear at any age, any time.

Also, don't think that the winner necessarily always finds his destination and stays with it all his life. He may change. He may decide that he wants something else altogether and if he does he has the flexibility to modify his destination or even veer away in another direction completely. *This is not failure*. Richer for his experience, the winner jumps ship and signs on elsewhere. Grimly sticking to a course which you have already decided is leading you to a destination you have discarded is not perseverance, it is mulish stupidity.

No, the winner may well change his destination, but when he does, it is *his* decision. Other people don't do it for him, he does it himself.

There is an old saying that 'Opportunity knocks but once'. Like so many old sayings, it's a lie. There is nothing carved in stone that says that opportunity will knock once for me, once for you and once for Charlie over there. Why should it? Life isn't so neat – or so fair and even. The truth is that for some the knock will never come, for others it will come only once and for yet others it seems to happen about twice a week.

Does this capricious practice of opportunity determine who the winners will be? If she (why is anything to do with good or bad fortune always referred to as female?) hammers on your door with the regularity of the phases of the moon, does this make you a winner? If she passes you by does this make you a loser? No, of course not. To run this metaphor threadbare, opportunity can be banging my door down, but if I am sitting in the back room whining at fate then I am not going to hear. If I am a winner then I don't sit around waiting for the knock; I go out into the street, grab opportunity by the throat and drag her inside.

All this means that the winner sees his own destination ahead of him. He looks up the track and sees the name on the station while the mob is still waiting for the train which won't ever arrive.

Carpe diem is a Latin tag which means, literally: 'Pluck the day'. Translated into the language of the winner it means: Make your own breaks. Don't wait for that unreliable harlot opportunity, she's working another street this week. Find your own destination, grab it, hang on to it.

How do I find it?

How do you find the destination you seek? Is there a magic formula? The best journalists, the ones who always get the scoops, have a reputation for being in the right place at the right time. But this is not what happens; how could it? What happens is that these people have a nose for a story. They see something which others pass by and they realise that the story is there, it's just that no one else has recognised it. This faculty has been called 'twenty-four-hour awareness' and all good newsmen have it. Winning salesmen have it, too; they see the prospect of a sale where other salesmen don't, and when they grab the sale under the noses of the losers the cry goes up: 'There you are, see? That lucky son of a gun just happened to be in the right place at the right time.'

Luck had nothing to do with it. The good reporter, the good salesman, simply grabbed the opportunity by the throat and made his own destination.

More examples? Here we go.

> In 1839 Charles Goodyear was doing an experiment with a mixture of sulphur and rubber. He clumsily spilt some of it on a hot stove and, no doubt, cursed the resulting mess and smell. Unlike most of us, he did not merely clean up, irritated at the waste of time, and start again. He fooled around with the goo and found his destination, because what he had produced was vulcanised rubber.

> Sir Alexander Fleming was producing bacillus cultures in a set of petri dishes when he noticed that the bacilli in one of the dishes were all dead; a mould had contaminated the dish. Instead of throwing the culture out he investigated; his destination was of course penicillin.

> The man who invented the simple shoelace made a fortune. Nothing very exciting about that, but wait; he had an assistant, a paid employee. I suppose that many men in this man's position would have envied his boss for his good luck of thinking of tying shoes up with pieces of string. Not this man. He looked at a shoelace and realised that it wasn't perfect, that something was missing. So he found his own destination; he invented the little metal dingus that goes on the end of the shoelace and made a fortune in his turn.

'Oh, come on, Beer,' you may be saying in disgust. 'What is the good of quoting great inventions and inventors? Do you really expect every ordinary person to produce a penicillin?' No, I don't, and we are indeed supposed to be talking about ordinary people. What about the character who worked in a menial capacity in the kitchen of a big hotel? An ordinary person – about as ordinary as you can get. One of his jobs was to open the big cans of fruit and vegetables and then lug the cans out to the rubbish area. The cans were a nuisance because of their bulk and they made the rubbish bigger and more expensive to carry away.

This man saw his destination in those cans. He went to all the hotels and restaurants in the area and made them a proposition. 'I will do you a favour,' he said. 'I will take away all your cans, cut down on your waste disposal problems, and it won't cost you a penny. All I ask is that you agree to let me have all your cans for the next five years.' His listeners must have thought that he was crazy, but they had nothing to lose and they gladly signed his simple agreement. Our hero then bodged together an amateurish gadget which crushed the cans into a truncated cone shape – a simple vase form – and he sprayed them with paint in various colours. His customers were nurserymen and florists who were crying out for a cheap container for pot-plants, and well within his five years he had made his first million.

Perceptivity, simple curiosity, twenty-four-hour awareness – call it what you will, all these people found their destination in life. Not by waiting for opportunity to knock but by going out and grabbing it.

Often, opportunity appears in disguise. This disguise is so cleverly done that the loser sees it as a set-back instead of a break. It takes a winner to see through the grease-paint and past the false nose. There was a man who as an employee of an oil company was having trouble getting together enough money to buy a decent house for his family (oil companies are not noted for paying exciting salaries to their rank and file). It was driving him crazy; every time he got enough money together for a deposit the price of houses went up. Who in those circumstances would not have thrown his hands up in despair at these continual set-backs?

What did this man do? He looked past the disguise, the

apparent set-back, and realised that what was happening was a property boom. He resigned his job and got into the real estate business (you can't beat 'em? Join 'em) and now he has his own agency and, of course, lives in the house of his dreams.

Anybody can do this sort of thing. The poorest, the most under-educated, the most deprived of us can see his destination and put his foot on the road that leads to it. No special talent is needed, no higher education, no dramatic IQ rating, no sparkling personality.

Desire won't do it

Lord Thomson of Fleet once said: 'There is only one formula for success – an overwhelming desire to succeed.' Correct; no question. But while this is the truth, it is not the whole truth, because something is missing here. Succeed at *what*? We need an overwhelming desire, yes, but what are we going to use it for? Where are we heading? It's no good getting down to the starting-blocks if we don't know where the finish tape is. Desire must have a destination, and that destination cannot be woolly or vague, it must be clear-cut and well-defined.

In my job I meet many people who have a sort of vague destination they would like to reach, but they have only the vaguest idea of how to get there, and not enough desire to find out. The other type of person I meet, and here is tragedy, is the one who has a tremendous desire but no destination. His tank is full, his engine is running, his car is in gear – he just doesn't have a road-map.

Destinations – or day-dreams?

For some reason which I can't really fathom I have always wanted to speak, read and write the German language. French and Italian don't attract me, and I wouldn't cross the road for the ability to speak Russian or Swedish. German, only German, is the language I should like to be fluent in. On my bookshelves there is a book on how to learn German, an English–German dictionary, a German phrase-book, and a set of language-learning cassettes. I have therefore accumulated all the paraphernalia for learning German.

I can't speak a word of German.

Why not? Obviously I want to speak German or I wouldn't have gone to the trouble and expense of gathering together all the wherewithal to learn it. I do want to. I should like to be able to read Goethe and Schiller, to understand German films and to speak with people the next time I go to Germany.

So why have I not learnt German? Very simple; I see my destination *but I am not prepared to make the trip*. I don't have the time right now, there are more urgent things to do, an hour learning the language is an hour away from my writing – I can produce plenty of excuses and they are plausible enough to sound valid. Plenty of *excuses* but there is only one *reason* and the reason is simplicity itself – I don't want it badly enough. Sure, I would like it, but I don't want it enough to make the effort and give it the time.

It isn't a destination – it's a *day-dream*.

And here we have the reason that so many of us fail to attain our goals. Even when we see the destination we wish to reach – when it is precisely pictured in our minds – we fail to get there because it is too much damn trouble to start down the road.

– And it's too much trouble because we don't want it as much as we think we do.

When I was much younger and even more foolish I remember complaining to a mentor of mine that I never seemed to have enough money to do the things I wanted to do. He smiled. 'And you never will have, Michael.'

'Well, thanks very much!'

'No, I mean it,' he said. 'You won't ever have a lot of money in your life. You may end up quite comfortably off, but you will never be what is called a wealthy man. You see, you don't want it enough.'

'What do you mean? Certainly I want it!'

'Not enough,' he said. 'You don't really have the *respect* for money which you need in order to accumulate a lot of it.'

Most people dream of riches, most people don't become rich. Why not? Because these are day-dreams, not destinations, and day-dreams never come true.

Not that there is anything against day-dreams, or I don't think there is. Why not have your day-dreams? Why not fantasise yourself on your yacht off Saint-Tropez or starring opposite Nastassia Kinski or having an irresistible personality or getting a phone call from the President of the United States to ask your advice? There's no harm in any of this, so long as we realise exactly what we are doing. By all means have your day-dreams; they are the Jacuzzi of the mind, where you can relax and drift aimlessly. I would not be without my day-dreams and I even have a special time for them. Up to my chin in a bath before dinner, the steamy vapours rising with the exotic smell of some bath oil stolen from my wife's special hoard, with an icy and very dry martini on the side of the tub – what better time to beat Arnold Palmer in a play-off for the Masters' trophy?

Only thing is that I have to get out of the bath sooner or later, and a good thing, too. Day-dreams are fine if we keep them in their proper place and know them for what they are – pure fantasy. If I, as it were, tried to stay in my day-dream bath for the rest of my life they would back the white wagon up for me and put me in a quiet place where I could day-dream for twenty-four hours a day and nobody would ever bother me.

That's the difference between day-dreams and destinations. Ten thousand girls dreamt of starring in a film with Humphrey Bogart; one girl named Laura walked up to Bogey and said, 'Mr Bogart, I'm the girl for your next picture.' She changed her name to Lauren, starred with Bogart and eventually married him. She had no day-dreams. Only destinations.

Make sure you want it

So, we have to distinguish between day-dreams and destinations. How do we do this? Isn't it easy sometimes to confuse the one with the other? Yes, it can be. One way to tell them apart is to ask ourselves: which are interesting, exciting and fun, and which could turn out to be hell on earth? The day-dreams are always interesting, exciting or fun. It would be interesting to be able to speak German. It would be exciting to be a famous public speaker. It would be fun to hob-nob with the beautiful people – so long as we don't have to walk the road to get there. Just thinking about these things is interesting, exciting and fun. But setting aside an hour every day to sit painstakingly learning German irregular verbs? Forget it. That wouldn't be a day-dream, that would be a destination, and the way is too rocky, the path too steep.

So we see that reaching your destination, while it just possibly can be interesting, exciting and fun, is far more likely to involve a slogging grind, hours and even years of effort, loss of

---

A test of what is real is that it is hard and rough. Joys are found in it, not pleasures. What is pleasant belongs to dreams.

Simone Weil

---

contact with your social circle, the giving-up of your hobbies and sports, and a complete disruption of your present lifestyle. Now, it doesn't have to happen like that, and many winners have reached their destinations without a ripple disturbing the placid pools of their lives; it doesn't have to be like that but be warned – it can.

[68]

So, before you head towards what you see as your destination in life, take a very careful look and *make sure that you want it*, and that you haven't been conned into thinking that this is your goal. It would be terrible if you set out to achieve it, if you tore your life apart and then with your objective secured, found that it was Dead Sea fruit, that you didn't want it at all. What an awful thing to happen!

I don't eat pickled olives. I don't like them. They don't taste of olives, they taste of vinegar. The thing is that for years and years I ate olives. People would say: 'Wow – olives!' And dive into the plate. I said 'Wow!' along with them, and dived in too. I had been talked into thinking I liked olives (especially those big black ones, you know? Wow!) One day it dawned on me that I didn't like olives – that I had *never* liked them. I had been conned into thinking I liked them because everyone else did. They tasted of vinegar. The hell with them.

Stop and think for a moment. Suppose you have a job with a big company. You are in the Marketing Division. What is your destination? Well, you want *up*, not so? You want to become Brand Manager then National Sales Manager then Marketing Director – the sky's the limit. The people around you who know you well think that your destination is along this road; your colleagues (who are probably also heading that way), your boss and your wife and family – all of them believe that your destination lies thataway.

But stop and think. Do you really like olives? Or have you been gulled into eating them because everyone else does and confidently expects you to like them too? Do you really want to be in the corridors of power, an important part of a big multinational company, calling the shots, affecting the destinies of hundreds of other people, with the money and privileges of a top executive? Or does the olive taste of vinegar, after all?

I have mentioned earlier how I realised that I was not happy in my job and how I decided to move out on my own – or how it was decided for me. I suppose that I had been conned into

[69]

thinking that everybody wanted to move up in the conventional way, so who was I to think differently? Everyone else was confidently marching in the same direction, so why should I hear a different drummer? Anyway, as I have said, one day it all jelled, and I realised that I didn't want what I was headed for. I bit into the olive. It tasted of vinegar.

Now you are surely too intelligent to believe that I am saying that if you happen to be in the same position that I was in, you should resign your job as I did. Your destination may well be President of the company you work for now. Don't think for a moment that merely because I looked ahead and didn't like what I saw, that I sneer at those who want what I did not. I'm perfectly willing to assume as a working hypothesis that I pulled out of the mainstream of business life and found myself a quiet backwater because I quailed at the prospect of what I would have to do to reach the destination ahead. Say that I chickened out, if you like; I won't argue.

One of my closest friends is one of those fortunate beings who has always had his destination clearly defined, and as it happens, this is in industry. He looked ahead at the responsibilities, the long hours, the awesome amount of travel which the job would involve, the interdepartmental backbiting, the blood and sweat of the business battleground, and he loved what he saw. He put his feet firmly on the road towards his destination and he has never looked back. He richly deserves his success.

No – I sneer at no man's destination. Romantic poet, clergyman, kindergarten teacher, political leader, army officer or postman – find your own. Just make sure that it *is* your own, and not something you have drifted into or been talked into or bullied into. 'You are a Beasley, my boy, and all Beasleys are lawyers,' is one of the dirtiest things a man can ever say to his son.

One of life's nastier tricks is to make you want something very badly indeed, so much that it fills your entire existence, and then after you have strained all your life for it, to deny that thing to you. There is only one worse tragedy that I can think of, and that is to reach your destination, bloody and exhausted after the long battle, and then to find out after all that it wasn't where you wanted to be.

Do you *really* like olives?

7
SELF-RELIANCE

You take the biggest single step towards becoming a winner when you accept the fact that nobody gives a damn about you.

Now, that is deliberately intended to shock you. If this section is to help you at all then I have to jerk you out of the comfortable feeling that grouped around you there are people whose sole aim in life is to help you get ahead, to pull you out of any holes you may fall into, calm your fears, boost your ego, encourage you when you falter, and generally fight off anybody who seeks to poke you in the eye.

Nobody gives a damn about you. Accept this, swallow it, gulp it down – and immediately become a stronger person than you are now.

Once you realise that everybody is far too busy with their own affairs, problems, deficiencies, hang-ups, terrors and calamities to bother about you, a wonderful thing happens: *you are free.* You are no longer saddled or burdened with expectations of assistance which in the crunch will not be forthcoming. You are not circumscribed by obligations of relationship which when real need arises will vanish like a snowflake on a hotplate. You are your own person.

You don't like this, do you? You reject the idea that nobody *really* cares about you. You can think of half-a-dozen close friends of whom you can say with complete confidence: 'Those people I can really trust. They would rally round if I needed them; they *care*.' Indeed? Friendship is a very pleasant thing; after all, what would life be without our friends? But the ties that bind are not nearly as strong as they look. Let the chains that link us with our friends lie slack and they will last a lifetime; put any undue or prolonged tension on them and they will snap. Friendship is a two-way thing and it blossoms between two people because of shared interests and a common approach to some aspect of living. You are my friend because we collect old coins, watch football, support the same political party, play chess, attend the same house of worship, read poetry or restore antique clocks. We do these things together; we have a common interest; we met through this interest and our acquaintanceship has ripened into friendship.

Take away that interest and see what happens. My doctor tells me to quit playing squash and take up something less strenuous, while you are on your way to becoming the club squash champion. You know what will happen; you and I will slowly drift apart. Oh, sure, we will still be pals. Swap Christmas cards, come to each other's birthday parties, clap each other on the back when we meet at charity functions; all that sort of thing. But what has happened to that close and valued friendship? It has withered on the vine because when you really come down to it we were not brothers, we were squash partners, and apart from that we didn't really give a damn about each other.

Strip away the sentimentality and you know that this is true. Prove it to yourself by thinking of your closest friend in school or college. You did everything together, didn't you? Damon and Pythias, right? One evening under the influence of a shared bottle you clasped hands and vowed eternal friendship. Now your jobs have placed you hundreds or thousands of miles apart (or even ten miles away, across

town). You haven't met in years. The occasional letter, perhaps. But apart from that how often has he been in your
thoughts in the last six months? If today you heard that he had
died, this blood-brother of yours, how would it affect you? I'll
tell you. There would be the initial shock. Then tonight you
would raise a sentimental glass to his memory and bore your
family with stories of the great times you and he had together.
Tomorrow? Tomorrow you would be irritated by the traffic,
happy about the new contract, concerned about your
waistline, and looking forward to watching Wimbledon on
television.

You didn't really give a damn about him.

All right, but what about your family? Your family really
cares about you, and here you are not going to give me an inch
in the argument. Let me insinuate however slightly that your
family is not bound by true feeling, love and affection, and you
will seek me out and beat me senseless. (You might do that
anyway, just on general principles; since starting to read this
section you have nothing but contempt for me.)

Well, it depends. In an unhappy marriage there is no caring
at all; in fact, as we all know, hate and revulsion grow faster in
a marriage than almost anywhere else. Let us examine the case
of a happy marriage, and I mean a really happy one, not one
where the partners stay together 'for the sake of the children'
or because divorce would be a disgrace or, as in many cases,
because of simple inertia. No, here we are postulating a union
where two people are held together by bonds of love, tender-
ness and mutual respect. This happens, thank heavens, many,
many times, and it does not negate what I have said before
because to all intents and purposes these two people can be
thought of as one. In a truly happy partnership such as this the
aims, ambitions, outlook and destinations are the same. They
are not divided, they are one. 'Man and wife make one fool,' as
Ben Jonson unkindly said.

Even in a happy marriage, have you never heard, when one
of the couple has died, how the first reaction of the surviving

spouse is something like: 'What will I do now? I'm left alone in the world! What will become of me?' And even the final accusation: 'How could you leave me!' These are the true, the immediate reactions, torn out of the bereaved one by the trauma of death. It sounds like grief for the departed until you examine it more closely: 'What will become of *me*?' What is this: grief for the dead, of a self-centred concern and anxiety for the living?

Children and parents? Parents and children? Yes, indeed, in a happy and united family there is love and caring. But have you seen love sicken and die when children have to assume the burden of looking after a single parent when they should be free to run their own lives with their own families? It happens all the time. On the other side, parents do help their children – up to a point and usually for the wrong reasons – but here again, love can easily turn to irritation and contempt if help is too frequently sought, if emotional blackmail is used once too often. ('I didn't ask to be born; you owe it to me!')

Nobody really cares about you. Hold on to that timeless reality. It will make you a winner.

What a monster the writer of this book must be! See him fighting his lonely way through the grey days of his loveless, friendless life, not feeling, not caring! By no means. I value my family far above any material possessions; my friends brighten my days as I hope I brighten theirs. Enjoy your family, enjoy your friends; keep seeking out those who think and feel the same as you do, who present the same face to life. Clasp them to your bosom, let them warm your brief spell on this earth; but don't jerk too hard or too often at the mighty hawsers that bind you together. They are gossamer threads.

The winner knows all this. He knows it is true and he prefers it that way. As a winner said to me: 'I demand from life the right to succeed or fail by myself, through my own efforts.' He has self-reliance built in.

When my father died I was shaken to find that all he had left my mother was a pile of debts and a life-insurance policy on which he had borrowed to the hilt. He had been an alcoholic and the monkey on his back had eaten up all the money. My mother walked away from the funeral and took up the reins again – at my age I hadn't realised that she had been running the family for years.

My mother had seen a long time ago that nobody cared. She never cried: 'What will become of us?' She simply went on with her life. She would have laughed at me if I had called her a winner, but winner she was. When my father was going through his bad times it was my mother who saw that we were well clothed, ate three meals a day and did our homework properly. When I realised what a financial mess we were in and with the ignorance and selfishness of youth I lashed out at my dead father for not providing for us, my mother shushed me. 'It doesn't matter. It wasn't his fault. We'll manage on our own.'

As I realise now, of course, the best thing my father ever did for my brother and me was not to leave us a pile of money. It isn't easy to become a winner when you are encumbered with wealth at an early age. I think my brother might have overcome this affliction; I'm not sure that I would.

The winner does this on his own. He demands this as his right.

When are you a failure?

I think it is time to turn away from the winner for a while and look at the failure. People do fail, and the consequences of their failures can of course be horrific; so horrific in fact that it is often the very fear of failure that keeps people from trying. 'Suppose I fail?' has kept many people from making the first move towards winning. Even now they sit and day-dream of what might have been if they had stretched out a finger to make that first move towards their own personal salvation. They don't make the move because of the possibility of failure.

[77]

But *when* have your failed? Who decides that you have failed? At what precise moment does the whistle blow, the

---

Nobody can make you feel inferior without your consent.

Eleanor Roosevelt

---

boom come down on you? I'll tell you, and you could do worse than write this in letters of fire in your heart:

You have failed when *you* decide you have failed.

You have lost your job? That isn't failure. You are doomed to walk on crutches the rest of your life? That isn't failure. You are flat broke and the bailiffs are beating your door down? That isn't failure. Nobody can ever point a finger at you and say: 'You have failed!' They don't know, only you know. You have failed only when you decide you have failed. This is not brash or slick, unrealistic over-optimism, it's the truth.

Do you remember Cecil the pest-control tycoon? Why did I label him a failure? Well, I didn't – he did. He decided he had failed and then proved it conclusively by killing himself. Had he accepted his bankruptcy, crawled out from the wreckage, dusted himself off and started again he would not have been a failure. The courts could have stuck the label of 'FAILURE' on him, his bank, his creditors, the big company which crushed him could all have dismissed him as a failure. None of that would have *made* him a failure. *He decided* he was a failure and that, and only that, made him one. You have failed when you decide you have failed – *and only you can make that decision*.

I must tell you about a friend of mine at school who considered that schoolwork was a rather silly 'filler' which the authorities had put into the curriculum between the important business of rugby and cricket. He was first team this and captain of that but his schoolwork tended to put teachers into early retirement. He failed this and failed that and he had to rewrite three subjects to scrape a pass out of school; the university accepted him only with the greatest reluctance. This reluctance was justified when he failed his first year so cleanly and completely that his professors were lost in admiration.

This character now has the sort of job where he walks into the office building and all he has to do is clear his throat and the entire staff goes straight up in the air in a sitting position and comes down busy. I once said to him: 'You know, buddy, I have to take my hat off to you for what you have accomplished after your history of failure.'

He said: 'What history of failure?'

'Well,' I pointed out. 'You didn't exactly have a star-studded academic career now, did you?'

'That?' he said. 'That wasn't failure.'

'Will you please run that one past me again?' I asked him. 'Why do you say that all those C-minus marks weren't what anyone could call failure?'

He said: 'Because in all that time I never thought of myself as a failure.' *I never thought of myself as a failure*. He knew that only he could tie the label 'FAILURE' on himself and he refused to do it. Even in the face of overwhelming evidence he did not think of himself as a failure and therefore he was not a failure. It is truly as simple as that.

The interesting thing is that in that same class at school we had a boy who came third from the top in all the schools in our area. Now that meant that he had a real brain. One supposes that after a record like that he would be on the first step of a golden ladder to an exalted destination. Well, I happened to bump into him a few years ago, and would you believe it? He has a sort of *nothing* job – uninteresting, dead-end, nothing. His general attitude showed that he was not getting out of life what his brilliant early showing should

[79]

almost have guaranteed. How did such a thing happen? I don't know, but could it be that *he thought of himself as a failure*?

The title of this chapter is 'Self-reliance'. Ultimately, you are alone. You have family and friends and business acquaintances and sports partners, but you are alone in the decisions you make about yourself and your life, in the road you travel to winning or losing. People don't decide for you, circumstances don't dictate to you; you do it yourself. You, and only you, have the right.

8
EXCUSES, EXCUSES

... Or, *'How can you expect me to join your crusade when you know I have this hang-nail?*

Sooner or later it happens to every man and woman. It can be triggered off by their first grey hair, by the realisation that they have a son who is eligible for his driving licence, or by seeing from a life-expectancy table that they have more years behind them than they have ahead. Whatever it is it makes them take another look at the small print in the contract. Slowly it dawns on them that nowhere there does it guarantee that life will always be fair, that it will go easy on them and give them the breaks. They finally understand that there is no free lunch, that the world doesn't owe them a living and that their guardian angel has left town and retired to the Bahamas.

Winners understood this years ago and reacted in the ways that made them winners. We are busy examining these ways in this book. Losers react in different ways, and it may be interesting to look at a selection of these; you have certainly met people who have used at least one of them.

The 'Goodbye, cold world' reaction

Some people kill themselves. This is the ultimate reaction to the realisation that those shining dreams of youth somehow got tarnished along the way. It seems a little drastic and the problem is of course that it is irreversible; if one does it successfully there is no turning back the clock, and what if, at the point of no return, we see in a flash of understanding that life, with all its disappointments and horrors and tragedies, is still sweeter than where we are headed? Is it not possible that in the microsecond before our eyes close forever, we would give anything to undo this final action? Except that we have nothing left to give.

It is cheap to sneer at a person so driven by circumstances and so ill-equipped to handle them that he takes the last and most private step of all by doing away with himself, but it is possible that many suicides are at least partly motivated by the feeling that 'They'll all be sorry when I'm gone!' It is natural and no doubt very comforting to feel that we are irreplaceable, that when we go we will leave an unfillable gap in the lives of those around us, that for the rest of their lives people will be filled with regret and remorse: 'If only we had appreciated him more when he was alive!'

It's a nice cosy thought but it isn't realistic. Apart from the suicide's immediate family the usual reaction is disgust at having to clean up the mess – scraping the pavement, hosing out the car, repainting the room – and irritation at having to tie up the loose ends. After that it is usually: 'Who was that clown who killed himself last year? Tried to gas himself, forgot to turn off the pilot light and blew out the kitchen wall.' People forget astonishingly quickly.

As far as one's family is concerned, it's a pretty shabby trick to arrange one's life so that people are dependent on one emotionally and financially, and then to leave as permanently as it is possible to leave; and a note saying, sorry, but at least I always loved you, is not much consolation.

The 'I never had a chance' reaction

This is the most common one. You could die of boredom reading all the variations. Here are a few samples, and I didn't make them up, I have had them related to me:

> 'I was pushed into this job; I really wanted to be an architect.'
> 'I get migraines.'
> 'My father was a compulsive gambler.'
> 'I had to leave school early – we were too poor.'
> 'I beat my brains out for four years to get three letters behind my name and when I graduate, bingo – a recession and no jobs in my field.'
> 'I had a nice little business going for me when they stuck a big import duty on my products.'
> 'Just as I was reaching for the plum job the company was taken over and they put another guy in.'
> 'Who's going to have any respect for someone who's as short as me?'

Recognise any of them? They are all variations on the same theme, that the breaks were against me, the cards were stacked, the ball bounced the wrong way.

These, the whiners, are the most irritating of all the losers. They are truly the small people, the trivial ones, and it is difficult to feel anything but contempt for them. If he is determined to be a loser then we won't try to stop him, but will he please go away and wallow in his misery in silence? We have other things to do.

The 'Don't blame me, blame my wife' reaction

This is similar to the previous reaction except that here the loser places the blame on those close to him rather than the bad luck which has dogged him all his life. His signature tune goes something like this: 'How do you expect me to make anything of my life when I'm chained to a wife and five brats?' (Where does he think his children came from – storks flying in relays? Yet thousands of men go through life bemoaning the fact that they have families.)

The woman who is tied to an invalid mother, the man who had to take charge of his brothers and sisters when he was eighteen because his father died – don't they seem to be heroic figures? And what marvellous excuses they have for not being successful. Only think what they could have achieved were it not for the burden of kinfolk which they so unselfishly assumed! Maybe, but don't you get the feeling that those burdens are a great reason to wave at the rest of the world (which is ready to be most sympathetic) as reasons to explain why they have never fulfilled their potential?

Not that they don't work, because they do; some of them work very hard indeed. The point is that they are not doing what they could be doing, what they should be doing, and that is what makes them losers.

This is to me is the mortal sin. If you have a talent for doing something well and you don't do it you are a loser. It doesn't

---

Look for your own. Do not do what someone else could do as well as you. Care for nothing in yourself but what you feel exists nowhere else – and out of yourself create the most irreplaceable of beings.

André Gide

---

matter if what you are doing in its place makes you millions, you are a loser, you have failed.

The 'That's the way it is with us Capricorns' reaction

Many failures adopt a pseudo-philosophical pose and ascribe their failure to predestination, the idea that their fate is written in the stars, that it is all part of some vast cosmic plan so how can you fight it? These people are easily recognised; they visit fortune-tellers, deal the tarot cards, attend seances, read the horoscopes and join the weirdo cults. It's a beautiful cop-out, this reaction. You can hardly blame me for being a loser if my fate was written 5,000 years ago in the inner tomb of the Great Pyramid now, can you?

If you saw a little part of yourself in any of these reactions then don't feel ashamed about it; welcome to the human race. We all have to look in the mirror every morning and many of us, in order to avoid ducking at the sight of that hopeless loser, make up the fairy-tales, build shelters to hide behind, and produce acceptable reasons for doing unacceptable things.

The difference between the winner and the loser is not that the winner doesn't have the failings and fairy-tales and shelters; it is that he sees them for what they are, laughs at himself, brushes them aside and does what he has to do.

The 'Dolphin or Bottle' alternative

Have you ever watched a school of dolphins at play? I don't mean the unfortunate ones which are kept in captivity for the profit of cruel people and the pleasure of stupid people, I mean dolphins free in the sea. I live near the sea and occasionally I have the rare privilege of seeing these beautiful creatures in the waves. They aren't hunting for food or fleeing from predators or going anywhere, they are simply having fun. They swim through the breakers, dive under them and – believe it – surf in them.

Have you ever watched a bottle in the sea? You know what happens to it. The waves throw it this way and that, they suck it in and spit it out again, they do with it as they please.

This is the choice you have; dolphin or bottle. The dolphins *use* the waves. They can't decide how big the waves will be, when they will arrive or where they will break, but they take each wave and decide: this one we will dive under, this one we will swim through, this one is good for surfing. *They* decide.

The bottle can make no decisions. The waves throw it around as they like. It is completely at the mercy of every ebb and flow until it is finally thrown out on the beach, rejected by the sea as something of no account or importance.

What are you in the sea of life – dolphin or bottle? Do you use the circumstances, the 'breaks' if you like, to your advantage? Or are you a bottle, being thrown around by fortune and misfortune, dependent on what tomorrow decides to do for you (or to you); hoping for the good breaks and dreading the bad breaks? You can't decide how big the waves will be or when or where they will break; what makes you a winner or a loser is how you react to circumstance.

These were dolphins

Thomas Carlyle had a tough break. He was dirt poor and desperately needed to make some money with the publication of his book on the French Revolution, on which he had spent years of time and effort. When he had finally completed the manuscript he gave it to his friend John Stuart Mill to read – and a servant-girl in Mill's house used it to light a fire.

I can fully sympathise with Carlyle's feeling when he heard the news. When I have typed the last page of a book I feel as though I have swum the Thames upstream, dragging the Royal Yacht with my teeth. I also never, never, want to see a word of that book again. Carlyle sat down and rewrote the book from start to finish, and it made his name and fortune. Why did he not throw up the whole idea? Who could have blamed him? He did it all again because he was a dolphin, not a bottle, that's why. He couldn't affect the circumstances, he could only affect his reaction to them.

A route salesman was so good at his job that he was able to buy a powerful sports car out of his commissions on sales; it was his heart's desire to own this car. He had a bad break when he crashed the car and smashed his spine. Now, a man in a wheelchair has a really good excuse for resigning from life. How can you point a finger at him? Well, in this case there was nothing to point at, because he came out of hospital and started his own business, and he now has five salesmen working for him in the company which he runs from his wheelchair. A dolphin, not a bottle.

There was a man who was chucked out of school when he was a child because the teachers thought he was either idle or stupid. In those days they didn't understand that he was neither, he merely suffered so badly from dyslexia that words on paper meant nothing to him at all. A secretary of mine went to work for him and she told me that she had to read all his letters to him. With no money, only a sketchy education and unable to read, what better excuse would you want? He is only the Chairman of his national chain of stores, that's all. What a dolphin!

A chance acquaintance once beat me in a game of golf. Nothing unusual in that; people do it every week. I out-drove him by fifty yards on every hole and he slaughtered me around the greens. He had only one arm, the damned dolphin.

My elder daughter won a national prize for her essay in matriculation; that is, she tied for first place with a girl whose home language wasn't even English. This girl had, in fact, won the highest award of its kind in the country, in what to her was a foreign language. At the prize-giving ceremony I congratulated the girl's mother on her brilliant daughter. She shook her head. 'No, she not very clever,' she said. 'She just work good.' The foreign dolphins are taking over.

Look around you and you will find the whole sea of life polluted by bottles. They are being thrown around in the waves with no life of their own, no part in their own destiny, no decisions about where they go. Look further out where the dolphins are playing – *using* the waves as they decide.

Dolphin or bottle? The choice is yours.

9

PRIDE OF PERFORMANCE

I live in a house which was built in the nineteenth century and while it has all the charm and character of its age, when you buy a house like that you automatically sign up for a crash course in electrical wiring, roofing, plumbing and plastering. When the downstairs toilet came clear away from the wall I found I had a mountain I could not climb, and I called in a plumber.

He took one look at the disaster. 'What you got here, mate,' he said, 'is a real old-fashioned WC. They don't make them like this any more.'

'No,' I agreed. 'There are laws against it now.'

He was wounded. 'No! It's a fine piece of work. It's just that I got to fix it in the old-fashioned way.'

I didn't have anything urgent to do so I watched him fix it in the old-fashioned way, which involved a blow-torch and a lot of semi-molten lead. When he had secured the whole thing back in position he began smoothing the lead with expert applications of the blow-torch in one hand and a grease-covered leather pad in the other. He got it looking very neat on the side which was visible and then proceeded more or less to stand on his head while he attacked the part which faced the wall. It was an obviously uncomfortable position and, judging by the proximity of the flame to his face, a potentially dangerous one.

I said, 'What are you doing now?'

He looked at me from his upside-down position. 'I'm smoothing this side,' he said, as if any fool would know.

I said, 'Well, don't bother. That's a hell of a position you are in and it can't be very comfortable. Save your sweat, call it a day, and thanks very much.' He ignored me and went on waving the blow-torch around within inches of his right ear. I said, 'Hey! That's enough. Nobody can see that side; nobody will know whether it has been smoothed or not.'

He turned the flame down and sat up. He said, 'I will know.'

I said, 'I beg your pardon. I didn't realise that I was talking to a professional,' and I went away and quit bothering him.

Now, I never got to be close friends with this plumber so I can't say for certain that he was a winner. All I know is that he had one of the prime characteristics of a winner; he had *Pride of Performance*.

What is Pride of Performance?

The job was done. The problem was solved. The owner (me) was satisfied. The smoothing-over meant additional and uncomfortable work. Nine men out of ten would have packed it in, taken my cheque, and walked away from it. Not this man; he had Pride of Performance.

Pride of Performance is a total inability to walk away from a half-arsed job. The winner simply can't do it. He can't do it, not because someone in authority will give him hell for not doing it properly; look around you and you will see many people grimly doing a proper job because of the unpleasant repercussions if they don't do it. That's not Pride of Performance, that's simply fear of consequences.

Pride of Performance, as with so many other characteristics of the winner, is a very self-centred thing. It has nothing to do with anyone else, it exists solely in the heart and soul of the winner himself. It does not depend on the approval or applause or acclaim of others. The winner does what he does because he can't do anything else.

My father and I used to walk to the station and catch the same train to town every morning. Regularly every morning he would buy the morning paper from the station bookstall and regularly every morning my father, the most polite of men, would greet the woman behind the counter with a pleasant 'Good morning'.

Now, I don't know what her circumstances were, what terrible demons inhabited her soul, so I don't judge her, but every morning she answered my father's greeting with a cold, fishlike stare; not a word, not a gesture, just this grim glare.

It made me mad that my father bothered to be polite to her, and one day I yelled at him: 'Why be so nice to her? She's nothing but a slob!'

He said: 'Michael, I don't do it for her, I do it for myself.' Even in such a simple thing as a polite greeting he had set certain standards for himself, and no matter what anyone else did he was going to keep to those standards. That is Pride of Performance.

Watch a long-distance event at an athletics meeting. It's the last lap of the Mile, and the leaders are beginning to make

---

You will give yourself peace of mind if you do every act of your life as if it were your last.

Marcus Aurelius

---

their moves. The crowd is on its feet, roaring its excitement as the three or four front runners battle it out for victory. Behind them in the ruck there is a perceptible easing-off; why beat your brains out to come seventh or eighth? Some of the middle runners even lope off the track, not bothering to finish.

Now look further back. There, a hundred yards behind the leaders, is a runner. Teeth gritted, muscles straining, he is into his final spurt. His only chance of winning is if nine athletes drop dead in their tracks but by God, he is going as hard as he can. He doesn't walk off the track, he doesn't fake a cramp, he runs as though the hounds of hell were snapping at his heels. By the time he gets to the finish line the show is already over and there are a few laughs and ironic cheers from the crowd. He doesn't care. His Pride of Performance would not let him ease up by 1 per cent; eyes bulging, arms and legs pumping, he crosses the line, stone last, going as hard as he can.

Does anyone doubt that in his own way he is as much of a winner as the man who walked off with the medal?

We see that Pride of Performance is another manifestation of the winner's complete lack of concern over the opinions of others as to his behaviour; he honestly doesn't care what people think about what he does. He has his own standards of conduct, set by himself, and he needs no mentor or supervisor of these standards. In any case, nobody could be as tough a taskmaster as he is over himself.

You have a degree of Pride of Performance yourself, in some field or another. There is something in your business, leisure

---

> Every man has to do one thing well. Not only well in itself, but well in relation to the way that other men do it.
>
> *The 17th Marquis de Portago, killed when a tyre burst at 170 m.p.h. in the last-ever Mille Miglia road race*

---

time or private life which you do well. How often have people said to you: 'Congratulations! That was terrific!' But none of the plaudits help at all if you feel that you have not given of your very best. You know that while it may have looked good to others it didn't feel right to you. Your Pride of Performance is not stroked or flattered by what other people think or say, it is something you have to live with all by yourself.

I have Pride of Performance in one field only. I have already described myself as Mr Average, and it's true. The only thing I really do well is my job. I do it as well as anyone I know and better than most. But none of us has all his plugs sparking every hour of every day of his life, and there are times when I step down from a speaking platform knowing that I haven't given of my best. People are polite, they applaud and they say nice things, but it doesn't help. *I* know the truth, and it's a long, lonely trip back home that night, just the two of us in that 250-seat aircraft – me and my Pride of Performance.

We see, don't we, that as with other characteristics of the winner, Pride of Performance is not an easy or comfortable thing to live with. It would be very much more restful and agreeable not to have it, to be content with the mediocre, the almost-as-good, the adequate, the acceptable. Nowhere here do I claim that the winner has a comfortable life. In many cases he is driven by a continuous search for perfection, not because of the wish for the approval of others but because he has this inability to live with himself if he has done only a 99 per cent job.

10
SPECIALISATION

A young widow found herself in need of extra money. She looked at herself objectively and asked, 'What have you got that you can sell, my girl?' Well, she was reasonably good at making dresses; she made all her own and those of her little daughter. The trouble was that a look in the classified section of the paper showed that there were hordes of women in the same position as herself, all advertising their services as dressmakers. It didn't seem that adding her name to the long list would make her rich.

She sighed as she held up a dress which she had just finished for her daughter. It really did look good, she thought; the smocking across the bodice gave it a truly professional finish. Funny how many women were good at dressmaking hated doing the smocking, or simply couldn't do it at all, while she loved it and was very good at it.

The light dawned, and a small advertisement in the local paper quickly brought her more smocking work than she could handle. She now runs a cottage industry with four assistants and she has become the smocking queen of the district.

What we have here is a winner who had the perception to

choose a smaller field to win in. There were dozens of dressmakers vying for business, but dressmaking is a wide field. Smocking, as a specialised part of dressmaking, is a relatively small one. This woman chose the narrow field and won in it.

A man with no more than casual interest looked up a piece of information on a type of snake found in his country. He was irritated to find that in the entire public library there was no book which dealt in detail with the snakes which inhabited his part of the world; they were all about snakes in Europe and the Americas. He is now an authority on herpetology in his country and his three books on the subject are standard works.

This is one of the easiest ways of becoming a winner. Don't forget that we are talking about the ordinary man and woman. The *Wunderkind*, the miracle-worker, the little-lower-than-the-angels character no doubt enters the widest field that he can possibly find and he ends up with medals, fame and the Nobel Prize. That's fine for him, but the ordinary person like you and me often finds his destination by walking a street so narrow that no-one else has even noticed it, let alone tried to enter it.

I don't mean that the potential winner makes his goal that of becoming the world's foremost armadillo-sexer, or the only registered marshmallow sculptor; it doesn't help to restrict

---

The secret of business is know something that nobody else knows.

Aristotle Onassis

---

your endeavours too much. That is the way to get into the Guinness Book of Records, but it won't make you a winner. All we say here is that it is often worthwhile *specialising* in some way or another.

[96]

Specialisation

Are you winning in what you are doing now, at this moment, or do you at least feel that you are on the right road to winning? Hang in there. But if you feel that there are just too many cost accountants or geography teachers or violinists or tree-surgeons or bakers or manicurists around then sit back and look at specialisation of some sort. As George Bernard Shaw said, 'In heaven, an angel is nobody in particular.' Heaven is a big place; lots of angels there and they are all doing good. Hey – over there is an angel *specialising* in looking after old, tired donkeys. See how his halo seems to have a special glory to it? A winner!

11
SELF-CONFIDENCE

Some years ago when my daughters were in their early teens I bundled them and some of their friends into the car and took them swimming at a large tidal pool which was really just a piece of the ocean with a wall around it. They piled out of the car in their brightly coloured costumes and were soon having fun in the shallow end of the pool, playing with beach balls, sliding down the chute and splashing in the knee-deep water.

All except one girl. She was about thirteen years old, a little tadpole of a thing, and she wore a plain black one-piece costume with a swimming badge on it. She walked along the wall of the pool until she had reached the deepest part. I watched in some apprehension – she was, after all, in my charge – but I soon realised that I had no need to worry, because she dived in with scarcely a splash and was soon doing a beautiful, relaxed crawl stroke and knifing through the water like a baby shark. Back and forth she went across this huge pool, turning each end with the economy and grace of an Olympic contender.

Well, in time they all came out of the water and walked back to where I was sitting for ice-creams and drinks, and as I watched them coming towards me I realised that there was something different about the girl in the black costume. It took me a while to see what the difference was; it was in the way she walked. *She walked like a professional.* There was just a suggestion of a strut in her gait, an arrogance, if you like, in the way she placed her feet on the ground, the way she held her shoulders. She walked like a professional. She knew she was good. Nobody had to tell her she was good, she knew it already, and the knowledge showed in the way she handled herself. She had the self-confidence of a winner.

It is astonishing how far the simple characteristic of self-confidence can take us. With it we are already in the fast lane; without it we are condemned to stay in the ruck.

Diogenes has always seemed to me to be the archetypal winner. He was a slave for most of his life and he never had a penny of his own, but what made him a winner was his

---

You know why that little guy beats you? He beats you because he *knows* he's going to beat you.

Tom Weiskopf, talking about Gary Player

---

incredible self-confidence. Self-confidence? Call it rather imperiousness or even conceit if you like. Any of those characteristics would seem to sit rather uncomfortably on the shoulders of a slave, one would think; let us see.

When the pirates who had captured Diogenes wanted to sell him they asked him if he had any saleable skills – you know, potter, iron-worker, farmer; that sort of thing. He said: 'Yes, as a matter of fact I do have a skill. I can govern men.' This from a slave, the lowest form of life! That's not all. When the pirate ship got to Aegina and he was put up on the slave block he pointed to a Corinthian merchant and *instructed* his captors: 'Sell me to that man; he needs me.' Can you beat it?

[100]

The Corinthian bought him and Diogenes became the teacher of his children.

He became well known for his particular brand of philosophy – he belonged to the Cynic school – and Alexander the Great came to visit him. Now, here was an interesting meeting. On the one hand we have Alexander, probably one of the most powerful men in the world at that time and certainly one of the greatest generals of all time; on the other we have a lowly slave sitting at the entrance of a large tub which he called home. Alexander in his glory said: 'Ask me anything you want and I will grant your wish.' Diogenes, in what must rank as one of the greatest squelches of all time, said: 'Will you please move out of my sunlight.'

Well; talk about self-confidence. Of course Alexander, who as it happens was a pretty conceited character himself, could have squashed Diogenes like an insect, but the *chutzpah* of the man so impressed him that he said: 'Were I not Alexander I should wish to be Diogenes.'

You might not like that story very much. It could occur to you that Diogenes was not all that pleasant a person – haughty, overbearing, abrasive. Right, he was probably all that. But recognise the *circumstances*. He was not born a slave, he had become one through a set of circumstances. Now, in that situation a human being has two choices: he can bow his head and submit to the dirty trick that providence has played on him (and what a lovely excuse he has for simply giving up. Who can fault him?). Or he can say: 'This is a straight fight between me and circumstance, and I am going to win it.' If he chooses the second then he is going to have to push everything else aside in order to fight the misfortune which has befallen him. In the process he will probably become an overbearing, haughty and abrasive personality. Mr Micawber with his unrealistic optimism and his 'Something will turn up' philosophy wouldn't get very far under those circumstances. That's not self-confidence, that's copping out.

[101]

Not that you expect to be sold into slavery, but if it happened you would have to draw on all your self-confidence to win.

The Eyeball-to-Eyeball Winner

One of the easiest ways to recognise a winner is to see the way he handles a head-to-head, one-on-one duel. This duel is fought not with pistols for two but with words. In the debate, argument or confrontation the winner wins because he has self-confidence.

But how can this be? Self-confidence by itself can't win a verbal duel when facts, logic, reasoning and judgement are allied against it. No it can't, but let us ask; where does the winner's self-confidence come from? It comes from the fact that, all unknown to his antagonist, the winner has prepared for the contest in one or more of three ways:

He has chosen the weapons.

He has chosen the battleground.

He has made the rules.

He has therefore as far as possible arranged the circumstances to suit himself.

A classic case of winning by arranging circumstances was the meeting between Chamberlain and Hitler in Munich in 1938. History tends to sneer at Chamberlain for his part in this meeting but in fact he never had a chance from start to finish. As British Prime Minister it was his job to try to persuade Hitler from turning Europe into a battleground, and he went to see Hitler to convince him of the necessity of keeping 'Peace in our time'. Let us see why he lost.

In the first place he went to the meeting with the wrong weapons. He took with him the regulation set of boxing-gloves, not realising that Hitler had drawn up a new set of rules which had nothing to do with the Marquis of Queensberry and that he was bringing into the ring a knuckle-duster and a cosh.

Chamberlain was vulnerable for two reasons. He didn't know that the rules had been changed, and although you may say that he was living in the past this merely intensified his vulnerability; he was still operating under the old rules of diplomacy and gentlemanly behaviour. Secondly, he desperately wanted to avoid war.

Hitler was armoured for two reasons. He had chosen the arena and made his own rules, and secondly and more importantly he didn't give a damn about the outcome of the meeting because he knew that no matter what was said it wouldn't have the slightest effect on what was going to happen. He knew there was going to be war *and he simply did not care*.

How strong our weapons are when we don't care about the result of the fight! We can call this the Armour of Indifference. When one side urgently and desperately *cares* about the outcome of the contest and the other side does not then the first side is terribly vulnerable. Diogenes won against Alexander because he didn't care, and he didn't care because he had nothing to lose. (Except his life, and he never seemed to worry very much about that.) Alexander seemed to be invulnerable in that brief encounter but in fact he was very vulnerable; his dignity was at stake, and it was his dignity which he lost in the end.

Let us look at how the Armour of Indifference can work in an ordinary business situation. Take the case of Horace, who joined a business firm in a time of severe recession. He knew very well that his job depended solely on the mercy of his boss and that he could be replaced in a second by any one of a dozen people who would gladly have taken his place. Horace had plenty to lose, his boss had nothing; in any sort of duel there was no contest, but of course Horace took great care

> Nothing splendid has ever been achieved except by those who dared to believe that something inside them was superior to circumstance.
>
> *Bruce Barton*

that there was nothing at any time even remotely approaching a confrontation because he knew that there could be only one outcome – he had to lose.

Then, as the years went by and the economic climate of the country improved, Horace was promoted to chief clerk and then to a managerial position. Slowly he began to gather weapons – his experience and knowledge of company policies and procedures, his ability to keep his people working as a team, his talent for getting staff to stay with the company even though they were getting attractive offers else-where (it was now a time of full employment, with companies swiping good people from each other). Now Horace's boss understands the situation very well; Horace has accumulated a formidable armoury of weapons which he could use any time he felt like it. His boss is sensitive to Horace's moods and eager to listen to his suggestions and complaints. The Armour of Indifference sits uncomfortably on Horace's shoulders at first; he has never been in any sort of position of power. It doesn't take long, however, before he decides that he likes it and that it suits him. It dawns on him that he could put his jacket on and walk across the road to another job where they would welcome him with open arms. He could even take some of the best people in his department along with him, in which case the company would be in deep trouble. This doesn't make Horace arrogant because he is not that sort of person, but it certainly gives him a self-confidence which he never had before.

More time goes by and now the balance of power swings, slowly and ineluctably, away from Horace again. He didn't use the weapons he had to force senior management to give him a higher position in the company, perhaps even a seat on the Board, and now his age is against him; also, young people are coming up with qualifications which he never dreamed of, and while he still holds his job and whatever title he was given in the golden days of his influence, he knows that he keeps them only through the grace and favour of the man who once feared his power. He has lost the weapons he once had, or rather they have become rusted through disuse. Once a potential winner, armoured by indifference to the outcome of any fight, Horace has lost his chance. The Armour of Indifference now sits back on the shoulders of his superior who wore it once so long ago and who has now taken it away from Horace for ever.

Why did Horace lose his chance of winning? Well, perhaps he wasn't *ready* to win; it can happen. I once watched a football team which was low down in the league tables play the favourites. It was generally agreed that they had no chance against the top side. Half-way through the game a weird thing happened; nobody could understand how it came about but suddenly the underdogs were smashing through the favourites' defence and putting them to rout. There was an awed silence around the field as it was realised that the tables were being turned.

And then an even more mysterious thing happened. The outsider team seemed to hesitate, to draw back, to stop in mid-stride. The favourites rallied and took advantage of the confusion in the ranks of the opposing side, and they won the game they could so easily have lost.

After the game many of the spectators discussed the strange turnaround of fortunes and puzzled over the sudden failure of what had looked like a winning side; why had the underdogs not capitalised on their advantage? Someone gave the answer. 'Easy,' he said. 'They weren't *ready* to win.'

No matter what the circumstances may be, no matter how much of an underdog he may seem, the winner is always *ready* to win. He expects to win, and even when he doesn't win in

---

It wasn't just luck. I *deserved* to win it.

Margaret Thatcher (aged nine) on winning a school prize

---

one particular situation he knows that he has given it his very best try and that he did not lose because he *expected* to lose. His self-confidence will not allow that sort of attitude.

To wind it up we could say that the loser loses, at least partly, simply because he expects to lose, and he is surprised when he wins; the winner wins at least partly because he expects to win, and he is surprised when he loses. The difference? Self-confidence.

Expect to win; it's half the battle.

12

ARE YOU BETTER THAN YOUR SCORE?

A man I know discovered the sport of ten-pin bowling and he rapidly became an addict. He put off an appointment with me in order to practise for an important match, and so when we did finally get together I asked him out of politeness how he had fared in the big game.

'Oh, I blew it,' he said in disgust. 'I was knocked out in the first round. What really annoys me is that I know that I'm better than that.'

What game or sport or pastime do you take part in where you can rack up some sort of score? Is it darts, clay-pigeon shooting, golf, javelin-throwing, snooker, archery or something else? How many times have you, at the end of the match, tournament or championship, said to yourself: 'Damn it, I am better than that. My score didn't give a true picture of my ability.' If you have ever felt like this then it wasn't necessarily bad sportsmanship; it didn't mean that you begrudged your opponent his victory. No, here again, as in so many instances in being a winner, this is something between yourself and you. What happened here was that you looked back on the game and said to yourself: 'I am better than my score.'

All right, but that was just a game. This is your life. In the game of your life, how do you feel? When you look back on your achievements so far, at your score, do you say in disgust as my bowling friend did: 'So far, I've blown it. What really annoys me is that I know that I'm better than that.'

Well, for the bowler the game was over; nothing he could do about it now. But your life isn't over, not by a long chalk, and if you feel that you are better than you are scoring then it is time to do something about it.

When? Now. This minute. Not next week. Now.

Yes, I know. Right now isn't a very good time, is it? You have things to do. I don't realise, do I, the many things which are standing in your way, so will I please stop preaching?

You think I don't know about it? Do you perhaps imagine that I haven't been exactly where you are now? Listen to me. I had to replace a piece of corrugated acrylic roofing on my carport. Now, I am the world's most unhandy handyman, and normally this would be the sort of job where I would let my fingers do the walking and call in an expert. It was only after five experts showed their lack of enthusiasm for coming out to do such a small and unprofitable job that I realised that I was going to have to do it myself. My lack of any aptitude, temperament or skill for manual work is no secret from my friends, and had this decision been broadcast they would have fallen about and probably lined up to watch the spectacle of me smashing my pelvic cradle and wrecking the structural integrity of that side of my house, trying to a childishly simple job.

Well, the days and weeks came and went and I didn't get round to doing the job. It wasn't that I didn't want to do it; oh, no, perish the thought. It was just that it wasn't a very good time to do it just then, you see, for a whole lot of excellent reasons:

1. I would have to borrow a roof-rack from my brother-in-law because the piece of acrylic

wouldn't fit inside my car and the hardware people wouldn't deliver.

2. I didn't have the proper type of saw to cut acrylic sheeting.

3. My drill bits were all blunt and I had enough of them to make it worth while to buy a sharpening tool instead of getting new bits. I was having trouble locating such a tool.

4. I would have to pull my workbench away from the wall to accommodate the sheet before I could position it properly to cut it, and the last time I did this I pulled a muscle in my lower back.

5. I would have to pick the right day to put up the sheet – it wasn't the sort of job you could do on anything like a windy day.

Those were the reasons I had assembled as my defence against doing the job.

Well, sitting back and looking at them dispassionately it is easy to see that they were not reasons, they were excuses. Hell, they weren't even excuses. They were the undergrowth, the garbage, the clutter which I had to sweep away before I could get down to the job.

The thing is I *needed* that clutter, I was desperately clinging to it, because without it I was going to be naked, with no excuses for not doing the job.

Not that it's important, but when my neighbour pointed out rather curtly that if a gale ripped off the old piece of roofing and took it over the fence into his greenhouse the resulting bill for glass replacement would be considerable, I realised that I would have to get rid of the clutter. What happened? Is it not amazing how when we do actually stagger to our feet, take a deep breath, grit our teeth and with our eyes tightly shut *do* the thing, the obstacles fade away? The sheeting fitted into my boot with only a little of it sticking out, especially after the hardware people had obligingly cut it to size for me. The drill bits were quite sharp enough to drill acrylic. The big day dawned with not a breath of air – I could have reroofed the Albert Hall standing on one leg.

I should have felt marvellous after doing the job but in fact I felt like a fool. What had been holding me back? Clutter, undergrowth, obstacles. It was only when circumstances had forced me to get cracking that I realised how trivial and petty all these obstacles really were. The three steps towards winning here were these:

First, the decision had to be made.

Second, the clutter had to be pushed aside.

Third, the job had to be done.

What are the obstacles?

How often do we see the task ahead of us and yet don't get going with it only because of the obstacles standing in our way. You are better than your score? All right, then you are going to have to do something about it, not so? Well, get going, mate! Ah, well, it's not so simple, you see. It's all very well to

---

Consider how long you have been postponing!

Marcus Aurelius

---

say get going just like that but you don't know the problems in my life which are stopping me dead. Not my fault, and God knows I'd like to get rid of them so that I can start scoring as well as I know I can, but just not possible; not right *now*, at least. You ask what exactly these problems are? You don't believe me, do you? Oh, you *believe* me but you want to know what the problems are? Well, for starters:

My father lives with us. I can't do a thing without him sticking his nose in and wanting to know all the details, and it just isn't worth the trouble.

I'm going through a specially busy time at work just now, and it isn't a good time to start anything new.

I'm having trouble with my tonsils and my doctor says that sooner or later they will have to come out, and this is really hanging over me and worrying me.

Look, don't expect me to concentrate on *anything* while I'm in the middle of trying to give up smoking!

All those people like you who keep advising me to go ahead, grab the opportunity – they make sense, I suppose, but they don't have to *do* it, do they? I'm the one who has to *do* it.

Recognise anything there? Does any one of those statements touch a nerve? You were quick to see through *my* 'reasons' for not getting down to the job – you saw that they were undergrowth, rubble, clutter. What are yours?

It is frightening to think of all the people on this planet who, right at this moment, are saying to themselves something like this: 'I know that I'm better than my score. I know that I'm capable of bigger things. I can build my own house, become a good public speaker, change my career path, write that novel, learn Italian, get the draughtsman's diploma, join the aerobics class, start a playschool, run for local office. I *can* do whatever it is I have been thinking about doing, *and I will*; I *will* score as good as I am.'

Well, what's stopping them?

Clutter: A disordered heap or mass of objects. A state of disorder.

Collins English Dictionary

You are familiar with the word Clutter and you will no doubt agree with those definitions of it. There's another definition in the dictionary which strikes even deeper: 'Unwanted echoes that confuse the observation of signals on a radar screen.'

– And the lexicographer who wrote that down was aiming it straight at me. That's the problem! In so many cases, that's exactly what it's all about! I have too much clutter on my inner radar screen, and it confuses my observation of signals.

I have wanted to write this book for two-thirds of my entire life. Other activities have intervened, big and small things have happened which have pushed it out of the forefront of my mind, I have written half a dozen other books over the years, but this is the one which has always been tucked away in a back room of my consciousness, up on a shelf, stored away for the right time. Every now and then I would open the door of the room and take the idea of this book off the shelf, have a look at it – and put it back again. There was so much else to do, you see.

Finally I found that I was irritating even myself with my continued procrastination. I began the elaborate process of tricking myself into starting the book. I know myself pretty well, and I long ago conceived the procedure designed to force me into undertaking any project which I was flinching from starting. The ritual is subtle, devious and tortuous.

First I looked in my stationery cupboard and found that I had only one pad of A4 paper, ruled feint, no margin. Well, one pad was only one hundred sheets, but normally – that is, when I was not writing a book – that would last me several months. When I'm writing it would not last one week. I went out and bought five pads of paper and stacked them on the corner of my desk. There they sat – lurked, not sat – condemning my dilatoriness. I got hold of one of those pocket notebooks with a pencil which slides into the spine of the book; very useful for taking quick notes when you think of them through the day. I decided that I couldn't stand ball pens for one more day and went out and bought myself a fountain pen with an exotic italic nib, and a packet of royal blue ink refills. I lined all this stuff up on my desk, ready to begin the book which I so much wanted to write.

Then I realised that my desk was not in the best place and that it never had been in the best place. Everyone knows that the light *must* come from behind the left shoulder when one is writing, or the most terrible things can happen to you; eye-strain, muscle strain, psychological stress – everything. Well, I obviously couldn't move all that heavy furniture by myself. The gardener could help but he wasn't due for three days, but as it happened that suited me very well because I had plenty to *do* before I did anything; three days was barely enough.

When we had moved the study furniture around so that the light was over my left shoulder it occurred to me that while the new set-up was fine for working during the day, what about the evenings? I had always wanted one of those cantilevered and articulated lamps which clamped to the desk and which you could move around to provide the *exact* amount of light at the *precise* position required.

I sallied forth again and eventually tracked down one of the lamps. (The first four shops either didn't have them or the colour of the shade was wrong for the study carpet.) I bore it home, clamped it to my desk and arranged is so that the light would fall on the work surface in such a way that it would give the best illumination without reflecting from the paper into my eyes.

There was one tiny snag. In its new location my desk was nowhere near an electrical outlet. I went down to the village again (I swear to God I'm not making this up) and bought three yards of two-cord flex, a coupler, a roll of insulating tape, a 15-amp plug, and a packet of those little things you hammer into the skirting to hold the flex in place.

While I was busy under the desk with a hammer my wife looked in at the door. She said: 'What are you doing?'

I said: 'I'm writing a book.'

She said nothing for a moment, then: 'Of course you are. Excuse me for interrupting,' and she closed the door quietly.

As I said, I'm not really a handyman; when I pick up any tool I somehow look wrong. After breaking three of the little plastic thingies and hitting my thumb twice I sat up and wondered if the best thing wouldn't be to call in an electrician and get him to install an outlet for the lamp behind the desk.

– Then I suddenly saw what had been happening in the past few days and just what I had been doing, and I began laughing. I roared and pounded the carpet and held my ribs. My wife opened the door again, looked at me, looked at the ceiling and closed the door even more quietly than before.

I took the lamp and flex and plug and all the other clutter and threw them all in the garage. I washed my hands, made myself a flask of coffee, sat down at my desk, filled my new fountain pen, checked the typewriter ribbon cassette, took the top pad off the stack, opened it and wrote 'Introduction: Who is running your life?'

Clutter. Our lives are filled with clutter. It obscures the clear signal we should be getting on our personal radar screens. It inhibits action. It provides the plausible excuses which make us score badly when we know we are better than our scores. Some clutter is self-induced as in my own two horrible examples (I *had* to do all those things before I could put up the roofing or start writing, don't you see?); some clutter comes from circumstances; some comes from other people – family, friends, acquaintances, strangers, enemies.

Now, if it is such a poisonous and dangerous thing, what can we do about it? We can simply be on eternal watch for it.

Constant vigilance is the only remedy against clutter. Watch out for it, recognise it for what it is and what it is doing to you, and sweep it aside.

There are really two types of clutter; internal and external. The easier of the two to recognise and handle is the external sort, that sort which comes from circumstances or from other people. The difficult sort, the internal sort, comes from within ourselves. It is self-induced. It is the nacreous covering we grow over the grain of sand which is irritating us into taking action. We resist taking the action because it is going to be time-consuming, difficult, laborious or just generally a pain in the bum, so we cover up the source of irritation so that we no longer have to bother about it, so that we can continue in the comfortable rut of the Non-success.

We are really quite clever at all this, you know. It's no good covering the irritation with clutter which we *know* is clutter because we couldn't live with that; it would be too humiliating. So we find different ways to go about hiding it which don't look like clutter, they look like *reasons*, reasons which absolutely prevent us from even thinking about the decisions we should take, the actions we should embark on.

There's nothing complicated or difficult about scoring as well as you are and you already know how to do it, but to help you there is a simple quiz at the end of this chapter. Fill in the answers and you are on your way – and you will have done it *yourself*, with nobody acting as your fairy godmother and waving a magic wand. This book doesn't pretend to have a mystical formula known only to the ancients and hidden for 5,000 years which, used as an incantation while standing in a pentagram of burning brimstone, will give you instant fame and fortune. You don't need anything like that. You already know the formula. You know what you want to do and what you want to be. It's your recurring day-dream; you have lived it in your head a thousand times. You see the road you have to take and the goal at the end. Only the clutter is stopping you.

A man went through one of my management clinics. He impressed me; he was intelligent, articulate and very presentable, and I had him pegged as one who was assuredly on his way to the top. I saw him three years later at an airport about to take a flight, but I didn't recognise him until he introduced himself, because the last time I had seen him he had worn a business suit, and he looked a different person now in his leather jacket and corduroy pants. He grinned when I asked him if he was on holiday.

'Hell, no. I'm going to a poultry farmers' convention.'

'*Poultry* farmers?' When I had worked with him he had been in the construction business.

'Sure,' he said. 'I'm a chicken farmer. It's something I've wanted to do all my life.' We had a cup of coffee while he expanded on his new life-style. 'I drifted into a commercial career and before I knew it I was doing pretty well, but deep down I knew that I was heading in the wrong direction.' Dear Saint Sebastian, I thought, that sounds familiar. He went on: 'Now at last I'm doing what I should have done from the beginning. I'll never be rich, Michael, but I'm doing what I want to do, my children are growing up in the country, my wife says I'm a pleasure to live with instead of the pain I used to be – I'm content. I should have taken the big step years ago.'

'What stopped you?' But I already had a good idea of the answer.

He looked sheepish. 'You won't believe it.'

I said: 'I think I may believe it. Tell me.'

He said: 'It sounds so damned silly, but I thought that everyone would tell me I was crazy, round the bend, fallen out of my tree. Can you believe that that is what held me back?'

I said: 'Only too easily. Tell me, what *did* people say when you told them you were giving up a successful executive job to spend the rest of your life up to your ankles in poultry droppings?'

He said: 'Well, Michael, that's the weird thing. Nobody

thought I was crazy. People stared at me with their mouths open and then they said things like:

> "What a great idea!"
> "I wish I had the guts to do something like that."
> "You lucky devil."
> "You're going to live for ever, you know that?"
> "I bet your wife is pleased."
> "You want a partner?"
> "You know, I've often thought of doing something like that."

'It was my own boss who said that he wished he had the guts to do something like that. Nobody said I was crazy. I *was* crazy – crazy to let a stupid idea like that hold me back from what I've always wanted to do.'

Clutter. When we recognise it for what it is, how easy it is to clear it away!

Not all of the experiences people have related to me have been so pleasant. A man had always wanted to be a dentist (don't ask me why; it seems an odd occupation to have as one's goal in life). His parents' finances were such that five years of university education were out of the question, and he went into commercial life. When he was twenty-seven years old he happened to mention to an old family friend that he had always had this dream of spending his life peering into people's mouths and scratching around in their bicuspids. The friend astonished him by saying: 'You can have it, if you really want it.' He was speechless. The friend went on: 'I have more money than I can use. I will stake you to your tuition fees and give you something towards your living expenses. You could take a part-time job, and with Nancy working as well, you could become a dentist.'

Well, this man chewed it over in his mind but he came to the conclusion that it was too late. He couldn't go back to sitting in a classroom with people ten years his junior. He and his wife were planning to have a baby soon. They wanted to start

---

The desire for safety stands against every great and noble enterprise.

Tacitus

---

building a house. His in-laws wouldn't be very impressed if he went off at a tangent like that after doing well in business. Clutter.

It was eight years later that he got a letter from the old family friend, asking him to come and see him. He went and was shocked to see that the old man had not long to live. The friend told him that he was a beneficiary in his will for a good deal of money. When he protested that he didn't expect anything his words were brushed aside. 'It's yours,' he was told. 'I tried to give it to you eight years ago. Do you remember?' The man nodded; he remembered only too well. 'If you had accepted it then you would have been in practice now as a dental surgeon.'

A cruel way, perhaps, to remind him that he had allowed clutter to destroy his dream.

The winner always recognises clutter for what it is, no matter how cleverly it is disguised, and he never allows it to keep him from his destination.

You can do something about your clutter and you don't have to wait a second. You have some time to spare right now. (Yes, you have, or you wouldn't be reading this.) Get a pencil and answer these questions. No, don't just sit there and *read* them; get out of the chair, find a pencil – it can't be further away than the next room – and start to fill in the answers.

Are you better than your score?

1. HOW CAN I MAKE MY SCORE AS GOOD AS I AM?

   Well, I can ....

   ....

   And I can ....

   ....

   And I can ....

   ....

2. WHAT IS STOPPING ME FROM DOING ALL THIS?

   Clutter No. 1: ....

   ....

   Clutter No. 2: ....

   ....

   Clutter No. 3: ....

   ....

3. WHEN CAN I GET RID OF ALL THAT CLUTTER?
   Time chart for clutter disposal

	START	WORK IN PROGRESS	REMOVED
No. 1:	....	....	....
No. 2:	....	....	....
No. 3:	....	....	....

4. WHEN DO I START SCORING?
   Time chart for scoring up to my ability

	START	WORK IN PROGRESS	COMPLETED
(a)	....	....	....
(b)	....	....	....
(c)	....	....	....

You won't fill the whole page in right now, of course; this is something you will keep coming back to in order to fill in your work in progress and to check on your results so far. Don't get carried away when you fill in the answers to No. 3; be realistic about dates. You have waited your whole life to start this, so take your time and get it right. The main thing, the whole thing, is to get it started and keep it *going*.

13
LAZY OR IDLE?

Scene: the Cash 'n' Carry Supermarket, Aisle Seven, Toiletries and Baby Foods. Enter PEGGY *and* BETSY, *pushing trolleys.*

PEGGY: Oh, I meant to ask you. How's that new neighbour of yours getting on?
BETSY: Claire? Oh, she seems to be managing all right. How, I really don't know, because I must say that she is the laziest person I have ever seen in my whole life.
PEGGY: No! Tell me about it.
BETSY: Well, you know that she and her husband and their three children moved into that old place less than three months ago. Now, you know what a mess that house was –
PEGGY: Mess doesn't even begin to describe it!
BETSY: Right. Well, wouldn't you think that she would be busy all day long, cleaning it up? I mean, it's not as though I've ever seen any workmen going in, and she doesn't seem to have a char, so anything that's got to be done has to be done by her and her husband. Not to speak of getting the kids off to school, doing the cleaning and washing and cooking and –
PEGGY: Oh, don't even talk about it!

BETSY: I know. Even thinking about all that work makes me want to slash my wrists.

PEGGY: And you say that she manages all right?

BETSY: Well, that's what I don't understand. She has put one of those lounging chairs out in the garden under that old apple tree –

PEGGY: Not possible. There's all that ugly shrubbery under that tree.

BETSY: No, all that is cleared away and the grass has been mown. Anyway, there she sits at her ease, reading and writing letters, wearing a sunsuit and sipping a glass of iced tea.

PEGGY: You mean, while she should be busy with cleaning and washing and cooking?

BETSY: Right! All I ever see her doing that looks in the least like work is when she picks some flowers from the garden.

PEGGY: Go on with you. There aren't any flowers in that garden, and it's not a garden, it's a cross between the Gobi Desert and the municipal dump.

BETSY: Not any more. There are masses of new plants in, and the fruit trees are pruned and the paths cleaned up.

PEGGY: Well then, the inside of the house must be a shambles.

BETSY: Well, that's the odd thing. They had us round for drinks last week. Peg, as far as I could see the whole place has been repainted – the downstairs has, anyway. I was quite ashamed to ask them back to our place. I mean, how am I ever going to find time to do anything about it with getting Charlie off to work and little Wendy to school?

PEGGY: Me too. And you say she just takes it easy most of the time?

BETSY: She seems to take it easy *all* of the time. I tell you, Peg, that Claire is the laziest person I have ever met!

PEGGY: Her poor family! Well, I'd better get on. *I* certainly don't have time to sit under apple trees reading and drinking iced tea.

CURTAIN

[122]

A fairly common and not very exciting scene – two women gossiping about a third. Suppose Claire, the lazy one, had happened to be shopping in the same supermarket and had been in Aisle Eight, Beverages and Preserves, and had been able to hear that conversation. What would her reaction have been? Probably something like this:

'Lazy? Why yes, I'm lazy. I don't see why I should spend all my life in drudgery, especially now that the weather's so lovely. It's so nice outdoors and my recliner chair is so comfy – and I'm getting a nice tan on my legs.'

Well! Claire admits to being lazy, and without any shame, either. How brazen! Let's have a look at the life-style of this slothful female.

She and her family moved into their house about three months ago. In that time she has repainted most of the interior, with her husband helping only in the weekends. She has replaced the cracked tiles in the kitchen and both bathrooms, scraped and varnished the banisters, made and hung curtains in the children's rooms, re-covered the sofa and rewired the chandelier. She gets her husband and three children off to work and school every day. She assists in playschool three mornings a week. She makes all her children's clothes and most of her own. She has turned the garden from a desert/dump into a delight, with her husband helping only with the big stones in the rockery. She belongs to the organisation whose members write letters to bedridden, lonely and aged people, and she does part-time voluntary work for the Animal Welfare Society.

'Sure,' says Claire. 'I'm lazy.' She means it, too; she isn't being funny.

Lazy? Yes. *Idle*? No.

Now, a thesaurus will give you 'Lazy' and 'Idle' as synonyms for each other and while that may be permissible in a thesaurus it isn't good enough for us, because there is a vast difference between the two words; at least there is for the winner. The thing is that while the lazy person can be a winner, the idle person is a loser first, last, and always. The difference, and we have taken a long time to reach it, is simply this: the winner is the master of time, the loser is the slave of time. That's it, right there. The winners *use* time. They use it as a mechanic uses a spanner, a musician a flute, a farmer a plough. To the winner time is a tool, an instrument, an implement. He has no fear of time; why should he have? It is the most useful single thing he possesses.

I must confess that this is the one characteristic of the winners which I admire and envy more than any other. These incredible people get up in the morning and they go out and do all these wonderful things and they don't even seem to work up a sweat while they do them. And then while everyone is frantically looking at their watches and groaning about how time has caught up with them and how there never seems to be enough time in the day and Oh my God I'm going to be late again and I was going to do so *much* today – while all this is going on the winner is reclining under an apple tree with iced tea, getting a nice tan on her legs.

How do the winners stay on top of time instead of letting time get on top of them? They do it somehow. In our supermarket scenario Claire was a master of time, Peggy and Betsy were slaves of it. What is Claire's secret?

I met a Claire once. I hadn't known her until then but I had heard of her, and from what people said about her she fitted Betsy's description of Claire to a T. I wangled an introduction to her at the conference we were both attending and by using all my fading charm on her I got her to open up. I said: 'From what I hear, you manage to put a quart of achievement into a pint pot of time. You do it without worry or flurry or hurry and you seem to have time to take it easy, too. How?'

She laughed. She said: 'Well, basically I'm a lazy slob. I like to have plenty of time to loaf around. Now the only way I can do this is to keep a very firm hold on my time. You ask what my secret is; well, I discovered something a long time ago and while I don't know if you can call it a secret it has made a big difference to my life.'

I was one large ear. 'Tell me.'

She said: 'I found that things take time when you *allow* them to take time. Things are greedy for time; it is as though they don't have enough time of their own and so they steal some of yours. People can be like that, too; have you noticed?

I said: 'Have I noticed! Saints and Angels, yes.'

'Well, when you allow that then time is on your back, it controls you and you never have enough of it. When I don't *allow* things – or people – to take more time than I allot for them then I am in control of time. Time is something I *use*, just as I use my food-processor or tumble-drier.'

Yes, she *had* discovered a secret. She literally commanded time, she was in control of it as a driver is in control of a motorcar or a foreman is in control of a working crew.

I said: 'All right, that's the secret. It's a way of looking at time which most people never understand. But it's only half an answer. You've said what you do, not how you do it.'

She said: 'Oh, that's not a secret. I just don't use tea-bags.'

I had the feeling that I had missed some vital link in our conversation, but not wanting to appear a complete idiot I nodded sagely: 'You just don't use tea-bags.'

She said: 'Right. Tea should be made in a proper teapot and it should stand and infuse for at least four minutes. So every morning I go down to the kitchen in my dressing-gown and I go through the ritual of boiling the water, warming the pot, putting three spoons of tea-leaves into the pot, pouring in the boiling water and putting the tea-cosy over the pot. Then I let it stand for four minutes, and in those four minutes I reach for the pad and pencil which always lie on the corner of the kitchen table.'

The penny dropped. I said: 'And you use those four minutes to organise your day.'

'Right. I put down everything I have to do that day, in any order at all; I'm not qualifying or classifying anything yet.

Then I allot some time to each of them. I'm not over-generous with the time I give them but on the other hand I don't try to be Wonderwoman. I give myself all the time I'm going to need without galloping through anything.'

I nodded. What Claire was explaining was a good idea, but there wasn't anything particularly magical about it, and many people organise their time in much the same way. It didn't explain how she managed to stay in control of time. She hadn't finished.

'*Then* I do my classifying. I *do* have a secret and I discovered it all by myself. The secret is to put everything I do into one of two categories – IMPORTANT or URGENT. Important things don't have to be urgent; urgent things needn't be important. Things can be both important and urgent, but most things simply are not. Now,' Claire said, 'the moment I discovered this, my life became a lot simpler to handle and time became a lot easier to control. I do it this way: next to my list of the five or ten or however many things I have to do I have two columns, headed I and U – Important and Urgent. Now in each column I put a number next to each item; the number may be anything from one to five. One is high, five is low. So an item which reads I–3 and U–1 isn't very important but it is very urgent, and an item reading I–1 and U–5 is top priority important but it's a long-term thing; not urgent at all.'

I said: 'This classifying really makes all that difference?'

'A *world* of difference.' Claire was emphatic. 'You see, just writing down a list of THINGS TO DO, which most people do anyway, can actually have the effect of spoiling your day before it even starts. You can look at the list and ask yourself in despair, 'How am I supposed to fight my way through all those things?' Now, with the 'Important' and 'Urgent' classification the list isn't nearly so long or as tough as it looks.'

'Why not?' I thought I saw, but I wanted her to say it.

She said patiently: 'Because some of the IMPORTANT things, if they have a low URGENT rating, can be left over to an easier day. This isn't simply procrastination, it is making order out of chaos. Now, everybody knows this but they don't act on it unless they have classified the things they have to do. But even that isn't the best thing that has come out of my idea of classification; the best thing is that even if a thing is Urgent–One, unless it is also high-priority Important, then if it doesn't fit into my day *I don't have to do it all*. Isn't that wonderful!'

I said: 'Give me an example of an Urgent–One, Important–Five.'

Claire thought. She said: 'I'll give you two, and both actually happened. I needed some flowers for the living-room. Now on Fridays the flower-seller near the post office sells her best blooms rather quickly in the morning because everyone wants flowers for the weekend, so if I want some I have to get there fast. But if my dear old Auntie Harriet gets on the phone she stays there for ever, and I don't have the heart to cut her short. So I don't worry about it, because although I am going to miss the best flowers I know that I can manage to find something reasonable in my own garden. Next one: we were going out to a formal party that night and I needed some dark grey pantihose to go with my black dress. If I was going to get some it had to be soon because there was too much to do later in the day. But if I didn't manage to get round to getting them I wasn't going to worry about it because my blue pin-stripe would be quite all right, and I had the right shade of pantihose for that dress. So instead of worrying about those two items I was able to scratch them off my list, and I saved time and bother. Both items were Urgent–One, Important–Five.'

I said: 'The interesting thing to me is that as you said, you not only saved time, you saved bother, so the items aren't sitting in the back of your mind, niggling at you all day long.'

'Right! And if I don't manage to do it I don't feel that I have failed in some way. I don't worry about it, and I have saved time to use on Important–One things.'

I was lost in admiration. 'And it allows you to be lazy.'

'It does indeed. Wow,' she said. 'If I used tea-bags in the morning I'd be in real trouble. I'd have no *time* to be lazy.'

So Claire was lazy. She was so organised that she was able to be lazy. The silly thing is that the idle person, as distinct from the lazy one, is forced into panicky, hectic, disorganised

---

> If only I could stand at a street corner with my hat in my hand, and beg people to throw their wasted time into it!
>
> *Bernard Berenson*

---

action when his haphazard life-style catches up with him. Then time jostles, badgers and bullies him, crowding into his space and showing him no mercy as it dominates his life.

The real winners fail to do many things. Nowhere is it written that they succeed in every enterprise or project or venture that they undertake. But at least when they do fail they don't ever say: 'If only I'd had the time!'

Examples of this are legion. Think of the students who work their way through higher education. How do they manage to fit in attending lectures, waiting on tables in steakhouses, and then going home and learning and doing their homework? What about the admirable women who turn out those paperback romances for the big publishing houses? Do you imagine that they all have two full-time secretaries taking dictation while they, the authors, lie back in bed on silken sheets drinking gin? Not a chance. Most of those people have a full-time job of running a home and bringing up a family, and they do their writing on the kitchen table on an ancient Smith-Corona portable, *after* they have done all the cleaning and cooking and washing and helping with school projects and bandaging grazed knees and bathing the dog and ironing their husbands' bowling pants – important stuff like that. They *never* say: 'I'd love to write a book but how could I ever find the time?'

They don't *find* the time. They *make* the time.

Lazy or idle?

Time is not an abstract, esoteric or theoretical concept; it is here and now, it exists, it is under your hand. Use it as as a servant, an appliance, a weapon.

Why not try Claire's secret tomorrow? Don't use tea-bags or instant coffee. While the leaves infuse and the filter drips, make out your list. Classify carefully – how URGENT? How IMPORTANT? If you do this as a daily habit, Claire and I guarantee that you will be the master, not the slave, of time – and that you will save enough of it just to be lazy.

14
RETREAT TO VICTORY –
THE EASIEST WAY TO WIN

I once worked for a man who always seemed to get his own way. Now, after all, he was the chief executive officer of the company, and one could say that it is no great trick to get your own way when your office has more windows than anyone else's, but the thing is that he seemed to do it without friction, without laying down the law, and without anything even approaching a confrontation.

I'm still not certain of just how he did it. Here's an example of how he operated; perhaps you can see where the magic was.

We had expanded into a new suite of offices and these were being redecorated before the department moved in. The paperhanger had arrived with the rolls of paper which had been chosen, and as my boss examined them he had an idea. He said: 'You know, Michael, this room would look much more spacious if the stripes on the wallpaper were horizontal instead of vertical. Don't you think so?' I hadn't given it any thought but yes, it seemed logical that vertical stripes would make the room look higher and horizontal stripes would make it look wider. I agreed, and he turned to the paperhanger. 'Let's do it that way, shall we?' he said. 'Hang the paper along instead of down.'

[131]

The paperhanger assumed an expression which I have seen all too often on the faces of technical people of all kinds. It is an expression which says: 'You are now on my ground, man. Here I am the expert and you are the fool, and I am about to show you up and in the process, boost my own ego at the expense of yours.' He said in a patronising manner: 'It can't be done that way. Wallpaper hangs down, not across, see? It's *never* done that way.'

My boss didn't seem very interested; he was looking at the floor tiles. He said absently: 'Well then, you'll be the first one to do it, won't you? Be a real breakthrough. Probably make you famous. (To me) Michael, what do you think, should we replace these tiles?'

The paperhanger lost some of his composure and with it his condescending manner. 'It – it would be very hard to do it sideways,' he said. 'And I would need an assistant.'

My boss, with his mind clearly on something else, said: 'What? Oh, yes, of course. Get someone to help you if you find you can't do it alone. Now, Michael, about the blinds – '

The paperhanger wasn't letting go. He said: 'Even with an assistant, it won't be easy!'

My boss was half-way across the room by now. He said: 'Of *course* it won't. That's why we got in an expert like you, instead of trying to do it ourselves. (To me) Will there be enough light in here with only those three fluorescent lamps?'

In that exchange my boss demonstrated the easiest way to win a fight, and that is, not to get into one, not to let one start.

What were his options there? Well, after the first sign of resistance from the paperhanger he could simply have pulled rank on him and said something like: 'You'll do it or I'll find someone who will!' This would have been an outright declaration of war, with only three possible results: the paperhanger could have hurled defiance at the manager and walked off the job, the manager could have summarily fired the paperhanger, or the job could have been done in a mood of what I have in other writings called Destructive Compliance. The paperhanger would have thought: 'I'll show that stupid bastard that you can't hang paper sideways,' and the result would have been a mess. No, a direct: 'Do it my way or get out' attitude would not have helped and no matter what the final result turned out to be, there would have been no *winner* in the confrontation.

Or, he could have tried Gentle Persuasion – persuasion as in sweet-talking, cajoling or just plain begging. That would have got the job done but it would have been done in triumph; the paperhanger would have been graciously pleased to accede to the manager's pleadings. The worker would have been the winner, the manager the loser; not to be thought of.

So in these first two options we would have had either no winners, or the wrong winner. The manager didn't like either of those so he played the scene so that there would be no *losers*. It is true that the artisan embarked on the job with his feathers ruffled and in a disgruntled frame of mind, but when the job was done and the new occupants of the suite came to view the results of the redecoration, it was the paperhanger who held the floor. 'You see that I hung the wallpaper sideways?' He told the group. 'You know why? Because it makes the room look wider, do you see? Hell of a job to do but how do you like it – pretty good, hey?' My boss was standing at the back of the group; I caught his eye and he winked solemnly.

You can win a battle – whether of fists, swords, guns, tanks, rockets or minds – in two ways. You can destroy your opponent utterly, or you can make sure the battle never happens.

I love nothing better than a tough debate with a bunch of hard-nosed characters sitting round over a couple of jars, with each one convinced that he is right and that the rest of the group are all half-witted. I don't mind what the subject is (so long as it isn't politics or religion, because those two can lead to life-long vendettas). One of the toughest people I have ever wrangled with is a man who simply will not fight. I charge into the arena waving my sword around my head, only to find that he freely concedes that I have a tremendously strong argument and that only an idiot would think otherwise. Then when I am about to accept the laurel wreath and the plaudits

---

The man who first raises his hand against another in an argument thereby admits that he has run out of ideas.

Old Chinese saying

---

of the assembled multitude I find that I have, in the rush of goodwill engendered by his apparent surrender, conceded a small but vital point which has made my standpoint suddenly much less logical and sound than it did. He wins by avoiding the fight.

Karate, kung-fu and the other glamorous martial arts have somehow tended to push judo out of the limelight, but it was always the creed of judo that you used the strength of your opponent to defeat him. You won by retreating, until he suddenly realised that he had confidently advanced into defeat, that you had retreated into victory.

Win the fight by not fighting; it's the easiest way.

15
COMMUNICATION

. . . Or, 'I've told you everything I know
– and you know nothing!'

I very nearly left this section out altogether because I do not want to seem to be insulting the reader's intelligence. It's so obvious, after all, that a winner is someone who is able to communicate well with his fellow men that to labour the point must surely be an exercise in futility.

To make sure of this I asked a dozen people what they thought was meant by the word 'Communication', and their answers made it clear that if I tried to write about winning without discussing communication I would be in trouble. What made me realise this was the sort of answers I got from the dozen or so people I talked to. Almost without exception they thought a bit and then said something like:

> 'Getting through to people.'
> 'Making someone understand what you mean.'
> 'Getting your message across.'
> 'Giving information clearly.'
> 'Telling or showing or explaining something so that people understand you.'

– Things like that. Well, that's all right, isn't it? Getting through to people, making sure that people understand you; that's what communication is all about, not so?

Not so. The winner does not merely talk to people in such a way as to make himself clearly understood. That's not communication, that's oratory, and the trouble with oratory, rhetoric and general speechifying is that it is one-way.

– And communication is two-way.

The trouble is that when we talk about communication we tend to talk *Transmission* – from us to those other people over there. We don't think *Reception* – from those other people over there to us. So we are concerned only with one-way when we should be thinking two-way, because the winner is above all things a great communicator and communication, unless it is two-way, is simply not communication at all.

Which is not to say that the winner is not an excellent Transmitter, because he is. One of the things which makes him a winner is that when he talks he usually says something worth listening to so people tend to listen to him. At the very least, he never waffles; at the very best, he sets the hearts of men on fire.

None of this means that you have to be Cicero or a Demosthenes in order to be a winner; you merely have to say something worth saying, and faults of grammar or diction, or a lack of a 'platform personality', are secondary to the content of what you say.

Four of us men were standing around a classic sports car trying to work out why the damned thing wouldn't start. We had adjusted, cleaned or replaced everything within reach and nothing seemed to make the slightest difference. A boy of, oh, say thirteen walked into the garage off the street and stared earnestly at the engine while we argued about whether the camshaft timing could be out. The boy took the last bite out of the apple he was eating, swallowed it, and announced: 'I th-think you have a cwack in your d-distwibutor c-cap and the sp-spark is shorting acwoss.' Whereupon he walked away, leaving four grown men staring at the almost invisible line running down the side of the distributor cap. Not one of your great orators perhaps, but an excellent Transmitter; when he opened his mouth he had something to say worth listening to.

Being a good Transmitter of course requires the very first characteristic of a winner: Knowledge. There's no substitute for it, you know. You will have heard the old saw (cleaned up here) that Bull Baffles Brains. It isn't true. Without a solid background of knowledge of what you are talking about, people will quickly see through the façade. The winner *knows*, and when he talks people realise that he knows, and they listen.

But that's Transmission, and it's only half of the story. The other half is Reception, and here we have an absolutely vital winning characteristic, because the most important half of communication is not talking, it is *listening*.

Have you noticed that people these days don't seem to listen? Why it is I really don't know; perhaps the tempo of

> The most immutable barrier in nature is between one man's thoughts and another's.
>
> *William James*

modern living just doesn't give us the time to listen. Perhaps we are so tied up in our little worlds that we shut our ears when people try to tell us things. Whatever it is, there is damned little listening going on.

When I was running a sales team I conceived a way of getting lots of prospects in a relatively short time. I got my salesmen to take one day a month away from normal selling, and on that day to make about fifty calls on new companies. All the salesman had to do was go into the entrance hall or lobby of the company, introduce himself to the receptionist –

she was his target that day; he didn't want to see anyone else – and say this simple sentence: 'I'm sure he's busy, and I don't want to see him, but who is responsible for buying electrical supplies?'

Now, that would seem to be a clear and easily understood request, wouldn't you say? Go back and read it over once more, please – see if there is any hidden difficulty in those nineteen words. Do you know what my men got in reply from the receptionist, at least once every three times of asking? He's busy; you can't see him right now.'

People just don't *listen*.

The sad fact is that we have grown accustomed to people not listening to us. We expect it. We have been conditioned to it over years of, firstly, poor transmission. (You get hopelessly lost because the helpful person who gave you directions forgets to tell you about the detour after the left-hand fork.) Secondly, we tend to approach the business of communicating with someone with the unhappy feeling that he isn't going to listen anyway, so we are half beaten before we start talking. This seems to be so especially with people whose *job* it is to listen to your problems.

My new car was coming up for its first 500-miles service when I noticed a little noise coming from somewhere underneath. Never mind, I thought, they'll fix it when I take it in and I tell them about it. Came the time for the service and I was received by a white-coated service manager who quickly took my particulars, tore the first slip out of my service book and said, 'Ready at five o'clock, sir.'

I said: 'Wait a minute – I'm getting a noise from under the car. Now, it seems to be coming from the – '

He raised a large hand to stop my ramblings. He jotted down: 'Fix noise' on my form and said: 'Right, sir; five o'clock.'

I went to fetch it at five o'clock. I said: 'Did they fix the noise?'

The man behind the counter, a different one from the morning, looked at the form. He said: 'They must have, there's nothing here to say they didn't.'

Well, I wiped the grease off my steering wheel and set off for home. No noise, but then it never seemed to happen when the car was cold. Sure enough, half-way home and there it was. I was in an irritated frame of mind when I got back to the service department next morning, and it wasn't helped by the frown on the face of the service manager when he saw me and said: 'Back again, are we?'

I said: 'Damn' right we are. Now look, let me tell you about this noise. It only happens when the car – '

'Don't you worry, sir,' he said, as though he was talking to a favourite but slightly dotty aunt. 'We'll fix it.'

They didn't fix it. I picked the car up that night, picked the toffee papers off the floor (I don't eat toffee) and drove home and there it was again. Now when I went back the next day I was as furious as I can ever remember. But what was the thing uppermost in my mind? I wanted the noise fixed, certainly, but that wasn't my top priority. Put yourself in my place and you will realise that what I wanted desperately, urgently, as a man dying of thirst wants water, was someone for the love of God to LISTEN TO ME!

I wanted someone to say: 'I'm sorry you are having this problem; it must be very annoying to have to come back and waste your time like this. Please tell me exactly what the problem is.'

Then I could say: 'Listen. It's a sort of a wucka-wucka-wucka noise. It only happens when the engine is warm, after a few miles, which is I suppose why your people haven't located it. It seems to be coming from the near side, under the passenger's feet.' That's what I wanted to say and I wanted someone to listen to every single word as though I was relating the formula for transmuting lead into gold or giving away the secret of eternal youth. I did not want someone, after I said three words, to brush me aside with: 'Don't worry, we'll fix it.'

Now it may seem that in this example I am merely indulging myself and taking time and space to get an annoying experience of poor service off my chest, but that isn't so. The point here is that the service manager, while he may have known the technical side of his job backwards forwards and up and down, will never be a winner. He may have knowledge, and we know how important that is to a winner, but he doesn't have the skill of communication because he isn't a Receiver. I never got close enough to him to know whether or not he was a good Transmitter; perhaps he was, but that's only half the story, as we all know.

What really and truly makes a good Receiver? One characteristic and only one, and it is the talent of Empathy.

I have changed my mind about empathy. Some years ago I believed – and put my belief on paper – that you are gifted with a certain degree of empathy and there's nothing much you can do about getting any more. When that book was published I was immediately challenged by more than one person on this point, and rightly so; I can't imagine how I could have been so

---

Great Spirit, let me not judge a man until I have walked in his moccasins.

Red Indian prayer

---

opinionated about it. We can indeed do something about increasing our quantum of empathy. We can become good communicators, which means good transmitters and receivers, simply by putting ourselves in the shoes of others and looking at things from their point of view – which is, almost word for word, the dictionary definition of empathy.

'If I were you'

So we see that the winner is both a good transmitter and a good receiver and that he uses empathy to increase his communicating skills.

You can do this and it doesn't require any special talent.

You can do it by using the magic which comes in the four words: IF I WERE YOU.

Say that you are in communication with me. You are giving me an instruction, asking me for information, persuading me to take some action – anything. How is it going, this interchange? If you feel that it is going well then fine, carry on with it, but if there is a problem of some sort, if the communication is not flowing freely and effectively then sit back and ask yourself: 'If I were Michael Beer, with his outlook, his problems, his deficiencies, his background, temperament, standard of education, experience and present mood – what would *work* for him? What can I say or do which would get through to him? Also, I am not only talking to him, he is talking to me. What is behind the words that he is using? What is he really trying to get across?'

Now, all that sounds complicated, and if we tried to go through a catechism like that every time we ordered a cup of coffee we would never get anywhere. But it really isn't complicated at all. It can be summed up in the four words: IF I WERE YOU.

Try it the very next time you have to communicate anything to anyone. If you were he or she, what would you say? How would you receive? How would *you* sound to *him*, if the roles were reversed?

There is magic in the four words. You really do walk in his moccasins.

16
RECOGNITION

Go into the general office of any large business organisation. Rows of desks, neatly placed one behind the other. Each desk has a head bent over a printed form, an ear attached to a telephone, a pair of hands flying over typewriter keys. What is the first and most lasting impression you get from the sight of all those people? It's probably one of *anonymity*. They are not individuals, there is nothing to distinguish one from the other. There is a facelessness about them. They are indeed anonymous, and this means that they will never be winners, at least not while they remain faceless, because one thing we can be absolutely sure of and that is that the winner is never anonymous.

The winner is *recognised*. There is no nonsense about him hiding his light under a bushel. The winner does not 'Do good by stealth and blush to find it fame', as Alexander Pope put it. When he does something good he makes sure that people know about it, and heavens, you and I know each other well enough by now to understand that by saying this we do not mean that the winner is a big-mouthed braggart. He doesn't boast about his doings, he simply makes sure that the right people know about them, that they recognise what he is and what he has done now and is capable of doing in the future. There is nothing anonymous about the winner.

We are still standing in that general office and let us assume that talent of ESP for a moment. We see that at the seventh desk in the third row there is someone who had decided that he/she will be a winner. Let us zip open the top of his head and look inside to see how he is going to proceed in this quest.

First, he sees very clearly that he needs recognition. He isn't going to get anywhere very fast if he sits at desk seven, row three, busily checking credit notes or adding up invoices or handling complaint forms all his life.

Second, our aspiring winner sees something else, and this piece of perception puts him ahead of all other people occupying all the other desks in that big office. He sees that merely doing his present job better than he does it now *is not going to help*. Checking more notes, adding up more invoices and handling more complaint forms is not going to get him any closer to being a winner than he is now.

Why not? Surely if he does his job better than he does it now his chances of advancement are improved? Suppose he determines that he will do his job faster (300 credit notes instead of 250), or more accurately (1¼ per cent of invoices wrong instead of 2⅛); won't that put him in line for promotion ahead of his fellows? Well, perhaps; and perhaps not. Nobody says that this is fair or just or reasonable or even logical, but the hardest worker is not necessarily the one who moves from one of those desks to the corner office, no matter what sort of business he is in. No matter what the Victorian romances say, talent and hard work by themselves are not an automatic ticket to fame and fortune.

Take as a classic example the acting profession. Now it is no secret that there are thousands more actors than there are jobs for actors in films, television and the theatre. One person is picked from all the hundreds who audition for the lead in a new television series. The series is a smash hit, the actor becomes a celebrity with his face better known than the Prime Minister's. What did it? Was it superior acting ability? Surely not; in the hundreds of actors who were turned down there were dozens who could have done the job at least as well and many who could have done better. The actor who was picked and who has now become rich and famous, unless his success has turned his head, is well aware of this. Clark Gable at the height of his fame insisted that he was 'just a lucky slob from Ohio who happened to be in the right place at the right time', and he wasn't being modest, he knew it was the truth. All right, he had talent, he could act, but hundreds of actors can act, and they are washing dishes in restaurants or checking your oil at petrol stations. He was picked because he was *recognised*, and he was recognised because there was something about him, no matter how small, that was different.

Seventh Desk, Third Row knows this. He knows that if he doesn't do a full day's work this will eventually be discovered and he will be fired, but he also knows that doing that full day's work isn't going to do one damned thing towards ensuring his movement up the ladder to the job of his dreams. He will be one of the people his boss looks at and says: 'Yes, good worker, seems to get on well enough with the others. What's his name again? Ah, yes; Ernie Something. Promote him? Now why on earth would I want to promote him? He's fine where he is.' Not the image which Desk Seven, Row Three wants to project.

So he works at projecting a very different image. 'Ernest? Ah, yes; Ernest. Good material, that man. If we don't move him up soon some other crowd will grab him.' That's more like it.

What does he do to be recognised? Well, we have already looked at some very powerful ways to gain recognition; we examined them in the section on Knowledge. Some other ways, since it always pays to have plenty of strings to your bow:

[145]

He is a problem-solver

It so happened that in the same month I had two of my salesmen telephone me during working hours to tell me that their company cars were giving trouble. The first one said: 'My whole working day is wrecked; my car has stalled and it won't start. What do I do?' I asked him where he was and found that he was two blocks away from a service station. As patiently as I could I said: 'Go to the service station, get them to look at the car, find out what's wrong with it, how long it will take to fix and what it will cost. Unless it's a major thing don't phone me again, just get them to fix it as fast as they can.'

He said: 'And what do I do in the meantime? How can I make my calls?'

'Malcolm,' I reminded him, keeping my voice under control, 'You are slap-bang in the middle of your territory right now. Within half a mile of where you are standing are some of your most important customers. Could you, do you think, take a small step towards justifying the exorbitant salary you no doubt expect to receive at the end of the month by using feet instead of wheels, just for today?'

This seemed to strike him as a masterly, if somewhat bizarre, tactical stroke. 'Why yes! I'll do just that!' said my hero.

My second salesman telephoned and the conversation went like this: 'Michael, my car broke down this morning, half-way through my calls. I phoned a service station to tow it in and got them to give me a quote on repairs. It's the rear universal joint. They weren't too keen to do it today but I persuaded them that it was urgent and it will be ready this evening. It's a flat-rate job so I didn't bother to get your okay on it. That all right?'

I said: 'Fine, Happy. Did it foul up your calling for the day?'

'Hell, no. I phoned my wife to pick me up, dropped her off at her Mom's place and I'm using her car today. Didn't cost me more than half an hour.'

Now, these two men were about equal in the performance

of their jobs. They did what they had been hired to do at about the same degree of competence. Territory planning, sales figures, credit control, paperwork – nothing to choose between them. But in my *perception* of them they were worlds apart, because in my mind Malcolm was a problem-bringer and Happy was a problem-solver.

The winner never, never, never brings his superior a problem without a suggested solution. Any idiot can drown his manager in problems, but if that is all you can do you are admitting that you haven't a single idea in your head and furthermore that when you walk into his office you are about to make his job and therefore his life more difficult and less pleasant than it was before you arrived. You are certainly being recognised, but it isn't the sort of recognition you want.

You have a problem to be solved or a decision to make which can't be done at your level? Very well, you have to take it higher up, but before you do make sure that you have some sort of solution to take with it.

Now of course it may be that your solution is simply not on, because of things which you aren't aware of; the higher-ups see a wider picture and there may be something which knocks your idea out of court. Even so, although the people at the top may have a wider view, those on the rock-pile itself sometimes have a deeper one. I can't count the number of times that one of my subordinates has come up with a solution to a problem which has been plaguing top management.

Still, suppose that your suggestion isn't feasible. It may be that your manager can turn it upside down, paint it green, add an antenna to it and incorporate it into the final solution, and you will have been recognised as a problem-solver, not as a problem-bringer.

Even if your suggestion is absolutely impossible, if it is thrown out *in toto*, you will be ahead of the game because you will have *tried*. I read somewhere where someone had written: 'There is no "try"; there is only "do" or "not do".' Don't you ever believe it. The winner is not a winner because he always succeeds; he is a winner because he always *tries*.

When I managed a working team I had problem-bringers and problem-solvers. Looking back now I remember the problem-bringers as an irritating blur, an amorphous blob, faceless. I remember each one of the problem-solvers with needle-sharp clarity. They were *recognised*.

He is not a yes-man

The days are long gone when you could rise in an organisation by laughing loudly at the manager's jokes, by agreeing with everything he said, by never having an independent opinion or raising your voice against his. Let nobody tell you different, those days are gone. If by any chance you are saying at this moment: 'That's wrong. In the business I work for you *can* get ahead by swarming around the boss and by being a yes-man' – if that is in your mind, then I have a piece of advice for you and I wish there was something stronger than italics to write it in: *Get out of there*. Run, don't walk, to the nearest exit. Find another job in another company where you work for a person who doesn't have the less attractive characteristics of Nero and Caligula.

No, the winner is not a yes-man because first, that simply is not his style and second, yes-men are never recognised. Yes-men are the chorus-line, the claque, which applauds every time the big man opens his mouth, and they went out with the starter handle and the separate collar. My job often lets me see both sides of some interesting stories. A man in an office department was talking to me about his chances of promotion, and he was highly optimistic. 'I have a terrific relationship with my department head,' he said. 'I'm really in his good books.'

He may have thought so, but I happened to sit in on the

meeting where the promotion was discussed, and this man's chances were killed stone dead when his manager said: 'He doesn't have a mind of his own. I can say north is south and he will go along with it.' Good-bye for ever.

None of this means that the winner is a rebel for the sake of it. Now here we have an interesting point. We have said several times so far that the winner doesn't go along with the herd, that he does think and act differently, that he stands apart from the mob. All very fine and true; he usually is a nonconformist; it is often this very characteristic which goes a long way towards making him a winner. But this doesn't make him a rebel. A rebel is someone who rises up against authority, and the winner isn't *against* anyone at all; he is *for* himself.

It does sound rather dashing and glamorous to be known as the rebel of the team, and most teams have at least one of these characters. You never know what he will do next, he chooses his own time to come and go, his style of dress is unconventional and he gets away with murder. The boss often has a twinkle in his eye when he talks about the rebel and it is obvious that while on occasion he drives management crazy, there is a soft spot in their hearts for him. This is because in spite of his rebellious attitude he is often very good at his job, and he is thus forgiven many sins.

Fine – *but he does not get promoted*. He may be a winner of a sort because he may be doing exactly what he wants to do, but if his idea of winning is moving up then he is going about it the wrong way. He is the interesting reverse side to our axiom that to be promoted you must be recognised. True, but recognised for what? Management may smile as they recount stories of the rebel's escapades, but they know that he isn't the sort of person they want in the job of running the company's affairs.

No, the winner is not a yes-man but neither is he a rebel. He is known for having his own opinions and ideas, as being the sort of person who doesn't accept things without looking at them from his own independent point of view; but at the same time he is not outrageously heretical just to impress others. We know by now that the winner does things to impress himself, because he is his own toughest judge.

He uses the person above him

I don't know what you do for a living, but if you have a job in a business organisation of some sort then, unless you happen to be the Managing Director, Chairman or President of the whole shebang, you will have a manager, foreman, director, overseer or supervisor in charge of your activities. One way the winner makes sure of being recognised is to make *use* of his manager. This may seem to be the wrong way round; after all, you were hired so that the manager could make use of *you* to hew the wood and draw the water and generally to play your part in furthering the aims and securing the prosperity of the company. True, but have you ever wondered why your *manager* was hired, and why he occupies the position he does? Why is he there, after all? I'll tell you, and it may give you a completely different idea of the relationship between you and him.

> *Your manager is there to make your job more effective.*

That's it. That's why he sits in that chair. Oh, he has other duties, depending in what type of department, division, branch of geographical area he may be, but in his job of *managing* he is of value to the organisation in direct proportion to how much better you become at your job.

Now if you accept this rather unconventional but realistic way of looking at your manager then when we say that the winner *uses* his boss it no longer sounds so crazy.

A copywriter in an international advertising agency asked her manager for some of his time to talk about a personal matter. She said something along these lines:

'Thanks for seeing me; I need your advice. I like this outfit and I like my job in it. I believe that I'm doing the job in the best way I know how, but that's only my opinion. I'm ambitious and I want to move up when I deserve it. Now, the one person on earth who is qualified to decide if I'm doing a decent job is you. You are also the only one who can tell me if there is any scope for the future. Now this is where I need your help. In your estimation, what are my strengths and weaknesses in the way I'm doing my job? What am I doing right that I can improve and what am I doing wrong that I can correct? This is the only way I can become more valuable to the agency. How about it?'

Her manager stared at her in amazement. 'My God,' he said finally. 'You are the first person who has ever said anything like that to me. The rest of the staff only come in here to complain about something or to ask for an increase in salary.' He pulled out two pads of paper and threw one across to her. 'Here,' he said. 'Let's get to work.'

In the next hour those two not only did a complete evaluation of that woman's job performance, they also set up a sort of timetable for future development, setting out key points and determining what to do about them. In the months that followed they had regular meetings to check on progress. I would love to say that she was promoted to an important management position within the year; I don't know because I lost touch with her manager (who was the one who had told me the story). No matter – she was the one who was *recognised*, and she did it by using the person above her.

What happened in that incident was of course an appraisal of her work which allowed them to set standards for the future. In fact that agency should have had an appraisal system in operation in any case. If your company doesn't have such a system, wouldn't it make sense to talk to your manager as that woman did? You can lose nothing and you stand to gain much. Whatever happens, you will be recognised as being that little bit different from the rest of the mob, and isn't that what this is all about?

'All right, suppose I do,' you say. 'Suppose I do exactly that. And then suppose he stares at me as though I was talking Urdu and either tells me not to waste his time, or he assures me that I am doing a fine job, just fine, no weaknesses, not to worry, everything is hunky-dory – the usual bull, in fact. What do I do then?'

Well, then, you are working for someone who is not fit to hold this job. He is not a manager of people because a manager is someone who builds people by guiding and counselling, and he is not doing these things. I mean this; if you really try to get him to do what that agency manager did and he resists it or ducks it then he is a terribly sorry excuse for a manager, and you probably don't have much chance of succeeding while you work for him. You are going to have to decide either to go over his head to more senior levels, which could be a quick way to commit suicide in that company, or to leave the company and find a job where the manager knows why he was put there in the first place.

If your present company already has a working appraisal system then approach the appraisal interview in the right frame of mind. Most people think of any staff evaluation system as a witch-hunt, to be used as a weapon to beat them over the head. Show your manager that you are eager to improve; encourage him to be tough with you when marking you under the various headings so that you can improve to the extent where he will be forced to upgrade you. Oh, you will be recognised, I promise you, because nobody at anyone of those desks out there in the main office has ever talked to the manager like that.

Never again will you be old what's-his-name at the seventh desk, third row. You will not be anonymous; you will have a name, you will have a place in your manager's mind. You will be recognised, and recognition is the first step towards becoming a winner.

17
ATTITUDE

Scene: The Koffee-Kup Kafé. Monday, 8.45 a.m. Enter ARTHUR *and* GEORGE, *representatives of two sales companies. They go to their accustomed table in the window and the waitress brings them coffee without having to ask what they want.*

ARTHUR: Nice weekend?

GEORGE: Well, it would have been except that my Saturday morning was a disaster.

ARTHUR: How so?

GEORGE: The sales manager made us all come in for an emergency meeting.

ARTHUR: (*shocked almost beyond words*): No! On a Saturday morning?

GEORGE: True as I sit here. Pass the sugar, will you? So that more or less wrecked the weekend.

ARTHUR: Well, I can see it would. But why have a meeting on a Saturday? I mean, nobody's buying anything, so why not have it in the middle of the week? It's not as if calling on customers would do any *good*.

GEORGE: Exactly what I told the manager. I said, look, it's not that I'm lazy. If I thought that there was a chance of getting any business why, I'd be the first out there, knocking on doors. But all you have to do is look at the financial news to see that nobody's got any money these days.

ARTHUR: Right! So what's the good of calling on people and wasting their time and annoying them when they aren't in a position to buy?

GEORGE: Thing is, you and I are *experienced*, you see. We know the market. I can pretty well predict how well I'm going to do in any week. Like for instance, yesterday I said to Maisie before I left for work: 'I bet I don't get a single order today.' You know what? I was dead right!

ARTHUR: Experience, that's what it is.

GEORGE: Yes, but you can't explain it to someone outside the business. Maisie just didn't understand.

ARTHUR: No experience, of course.

GEORGE: None. So she says: 'George, you sell microwave ovens to shops. Well, people are buying microwaves every

---

There are no hopeless situations; there are only men who have grown hopeless about them.

Clare Booth Luce

---

day. Ken and Barbie next door bought one only last week. Well,' she says in her innocence, 'if people are buying them then your customers must be selling them, which means that they must be buying more of them from *someone* to sell again.'

ARTHUR: Ah, you can't explain to an outsider.

GEORGE: They just don't understand. Mind, I'm not saying Maisie's stupid; she just doesn't see that it isn't as simple as all that. Thing is, my sales manager, who should know better, has fallen into the same trap as Maisie. He seems to think you can go out and find business when the market is stone dead.

ARTHUR: I've got one like that, too. I told him, why should I ride around wasting the firm's petrol when my experience tells me that the business just isn't there? (He glances out of the window) George – isn't that one of your company's cars going by? I thought I saw the logo on the door.

GEORGE: Where? Oh, yes; that'll be young Ernie.

ARTHUR: Where's he going at this time in the morning?

GEORGE: On his way to see some customers, I suppose.

ARTHUR (*horrified at this blasphemy*): What, before ten o'clock? Go on! You should tell him that you can't call on people so early in the morning.

GEORGE: I've told him a dozen times. He can't see that it irritates people if you burst in on them before they have got their breath.

ARTHUR: Well, you should take him under your wing and help him with the benefit of your experience.

GEORGE: I tell you, I've *tried*. Look at him now, rushing around as if he was accomplishing something. Do you know, he told me that he had made thirteen calls on Friday. On *Friday*, if you don't mind.

ARTHUR (*almost speechless*): Well, that's it. If he doesn't know that Friday is a bad day to see people then I'm afraid he's stupid. Sorry to say it but there it is.

GEORGE: No, Arthur, you're right. I have to admit that he *is* stupid. Lord only knows how he's going to cope in Greece.

ARTHUR: Greece? What's he going to Greece for?

GEORGE: Oh, we had this sales contest last month and he managed to win it, don't ask me how. Must have walked into a couple of fluke orders at the right time.

ARTHUR: Lucky!

GEORGE: Just lucky. Another cuppa?

ARTHUR: Might as well. No point in rushing around, working up a sweat, is there?

GEORGE: No point at all.

Attitude. Finally, when the tumult and the shouting dies, it all comes down to this, doesn't it? Everything depends on the attitude with which we approach, handle and overcome the problems of living.

You know, it is frightening to realise that we have *complete* control over almost nothing. As one individual human being, what do you control completely? What is in your power to alter?

You have no control whatever over the weather, the international economic situation, the chances of global war, the ozone layer, the dwindling supply of fossil fuels, or the stockpiling of radioactive waste.

You have at best only very limited control over your resistance to disease, the sort of people who govern your country, your vulnerability to mugging, your intelligence quotient, or your chances of being hijacked in an aircraft.

– All of which looks very much as if you are a bottle in the sea of life, doesn't it? To the first question in this book, 'Who is running your life?', it seems that the answer is: 'Other people; fate, predestination, kismet, and other people.'

Yes – and no. Yes, because so many things are indeed beyond your control. No, because you do have, at all times and in all situations, complete and absolute control of your *attitude*. It is awesome to think that it is the *only* thing you control entirely, and since this is so it must follow *that the only real difference between the winner and the loser is attitude*.

I see the truth of this in my job. I am sometimes asked to sit in on staff selection meetings, where people are being considered for recruitment or promotion. Now, let us suppose that you and I are thinking of taking on a person for some job in our company. What would we want this person to be, to look like, to have? Our list could look something like this:

APPEARANCE: while looks aren't everything, we would want him at least not to disgrace our organisation by coming to work looking as though he has just lost an argument with a grizzly bear.

HONESTY: we shouldn't even have to put this down, it should go without saying, but it sometimes doesn't so down it goes.

KNOWLEDGE: we had this as one of the prime characteristics of the winner and we can't leave it out here.

EXPERIENCE: not essential, but it always makes it easier to get him going if he isn't completely green.

EMPATHY: another characteristic of the winner, and how much more valuable he will be to us if he can get on with people and look at things from their side of the situation.

HEALTH: physically and mentally healthy? Of course.

ENERGY: this aspect contradicts nothing which we said in the chapter 'Lazy or Idle'. There will be times when he will need all the energy he has.

Well, that may not be a complete or exhaustive list but it will do for a start. One would think that someone with all those attributes would stand a pretty good chance of succeeding in any job we are going to give him, right?

Perhaps, but do you know, I regularly meet people and work with them and find that they are good-looking, honest, knowledgeable, experienced, empathetic, healthy, energetic, *failures*. They have it all and they are still not winners. The tank is full, the tyres are pumped up, the engine is tuned, the battery is fully charged; nothing happens because there is no key.

The key is attitude. Without it, no go.

You and I have come too far together for you to think that when I say 'Attitude' I am talking about pie-in-the-sky, unrealistic optimism. The people who give you the 'It will be a brighter day tomorrow, it's always darkest before the dawn, every cloud has a silver lining' guff merely irritate you or make you wonder if they have been too hastily assembled. The 'Anybody can do anything' school lack credibility because when you look them over you often realise that most of them can't really do anything much at all.

No, of course you can't do everything. Physical, mental and inherent characteristics will always restrict us, and a good thing too. But remember the old Spanish saying: 'Be careful what you pray for; you will probably get it.' What this means is that if you want something, want it so badly that it sits on your pillow when you go to sleep and is still there as you open your eyes in the morning, and if it is truly a destination and not a day-dream, then you will do the things and be the things that ensure that you will probably get it.

An interesting point here is that you probably won't get any *more* than you want, because you probably won't do any more than is necessary to get what you want. I am thinking of two sportsmen and I can't name them because they are both very much alive and I don't want to embarrass them. They both came from lowly backgrounds and they were both fired with a single-mindedness of purpose which is so often the characteristic of the winner; each one had his destination clear in his mind, although each was different. X, having been born into a poor family, wanted to be a millionaire. Y, having been born into a humble family, wanted to be world-famous. They both chose the same sport as the road to their destinations.

What happened? What do you think happened? They got exactly what they wanted. X quickly rose to the top in his chosen field, won a couple of international tournaments and got his millions. Since then, although he still plays, he has faded back into the also-rans. Y became one of the immortals in his chosen field; his name will be mentioned as long as the game is played. As it happened he also became very rich, but that was truly incidental to the fame.

Attitude

You get what you really want; realistically, constructively, pragmatically want, and it is your attitude and only your attitude which decides this.

That's a very positive statement; one of the most positive that you have read in these pages. It is not unrealistically optimistic, though; no matter how positive we are we must at all times keep a firm grasp on reality. So long as we do this we can be – must be – as positive as we know how. Without this everything looks murky.

I was buttonholed by a man at a party I had tried to duck out of and forced into a conversation I didn't want any part

> The greatest revolution of our generation is the discovery that human beings, by changing the inner attitudes of their minds, can change the outer aspects of their lives.
>
> *William James*

of. He mentioned the name of the company where he was employed and I said, just for something to say: 'Oh, yes; that's a good crowd, I hear. Are you happy there?' Not that I cared.

He said, frowning: 'No, as a matter of fact I'm just marking time until I find a *good* place.'

I said: 'What's wrong with your present company?' Now I *was* interested because I had a feeling that I had played this scene before with many different actors opposite me.

He said, as if it explained everything: 'Well, it's got *problems*, you see.'

Well, it so happened that a few months later I was introduced to two men and it turned out that they were from the same company as the first man. I thought I might as well do some research on my fellow man and I asked them: 'What's it like, working in your company?'

[159]

One of them said: 'Why, it's fine. Good people,' and his colleague nodded in confirmation.

I said: 'No – *problems*?'

They looked mildly surprised. One said; 'Problems? Well, of course there are *problems*. But to look at it one way, you could say that one of the reasons we were hired was because of problems. Without problems a company wouldn't need particularly good people.'

The other man said: 'Did you ever hear of a company which didn't have problems?'

I said: 'No, as a matter of fact I never did.'

It all comes down to attitude.

In a sales clinic I was handling the problem of sales resistance. One of the delegates said: 'Hell! What an easy job I would have if nobody raised an objection!'

What do you say to an attitude like that? I was spared the job of thinking up something to say which would straighten him out without squashing him when a delegate said: 'Chum, if nobody ever raised an objection you and I would be out of a job. That's what we were hired for – to handle them!'

Attitude!

There's not much else to say. I have tried to show that you don't have to be a superman to be a winner; that there is no magical ingredient in winning; that winners can be very ordinary people. If I have come across in these writings as a sort of one-man commando platoon, as a very positive person, then I'm sorry, because it isn't like that at all. The truth is that I have always been negative-minded – *and I still am*. For me the bottle will always be half-empty already, never still half-full. I realised something a long time ago and if you are negative-minded like me it may hit you like a thunderbolt, as it did me. Here it is:

You are as successful as you *allow* yourself to be. What stops you winning is not fate, providence, fortune, chance or circumstance. *You* are the only thing stopping you from winning.

Allow yourself to win.

INDEX

alcoholics, 53, 77
Alexander the Great, 101
Alliance Français, 22
Armour of Indifference, 103
Aurelius, Marcus, 91, 110
Average, John, 6, 93
averages, law of, 51

Bacall, Lauren, 67
Barton, Bruce, 104
Beerbohm, Max, 37
Berenson, Bernard, 128
better than your score, 119
blame, 83
Boadicea, 59
Bogart, Humphrey, 67
Bolívar, 59
bowler, 17
boxer, 17

Capricorns, 85
Carlyle, Thomas, 86
Catch-22, 33
Chamberlain, 102

chance, never had, 83
chicken-egg situation, 9
Chinese saying, 134
Cicero, 136
clutter, 112
courage, 51

Damon and Pythias, 74
daydreams, 66
Demosthenes, 136
destructive compliance, 132
dictating machine salesman, 56
Diogenes, 100
dophin or bottle, 85
dyslexia, 87

Edison, Thomas Alva, 11
empathy, 140
enemy, knowledge of, 13
ESP, 144
Evert, Chris, 28
eyeball-to-eyeball, 102

failure, 41, 42

Fleming, Alexander, 63
football, 17

Gable, Clark, 145
Garibaldi, 59
gentle persuasion, 133
German language, 65
Gide, André, 84
Gobi Desert, 122
Goethe, 27
Goodyear, Charles, 63
Graf, Steffi, 36

Harrison, Frederic, 19
Hitler, Adolf, 102
Hockney, David, 36

Iacocca, Lee, 36
important or urgent, 126

Jaeger, Andrea, 28
James, William, 137, 159
Johnson, Samuel, 20
Jonson, Ben, 75

Killer Instinct, 27
Kinski, Nastassia, 67
knowledge, 11
knowledge with action, 25

life insurance salesman, 14
loser, good, 27
Luce, Clare Booth, 154
Luther, 59

market research companies, 18
marketing companies, 17
Micawber, Mr, 101
Mill, John Stuart, 86
Morley, Christopher, 9
Moses, 59

nice guys, 32
Nicklaus, Jack, 34
Non-success, 41

Old Boy, 35
olives, pickled, 69
Onassis, Aristotle, 96
opportunity, 61

Palmer, Arnold, 67
paperhanger, 131
pattern of winning, 7, 9
penicillin, 63
pest-control company, 42, 78
Player, Gary, 34, 100
plumber, 89
politician, 17
poor boy – rich boy, 33
Pope, Alexander, 143
Portago, Marquis de, 92
poultry farmer, 116
problem-solver, 146
professional, walk like, 100

Queensberry, Marquis of, 103

reception, 136
Red Indian prayer, 140
Roosevelt, Eleanor, 78
roulette wheel, 51

Santayana, George, 49
Shaw, George Bernard, 97
Smith, Wilbur, 36
smocking, 95
snakes, 96
space salesman, 48
spiral, descending, 55
success books, 4
Success, the 41

suicide, 82
Superman, 7, 8, 9, 18

Tacitus, 118
Thatcher, Margaret, 36, 106
Thomson, Lord of Fleet, 65
Thoreau, Henry, 4
transmission, 136
twenty-four-hour awareness, 62

wasting time, 23
Weil, Simone, 68
Weiskopf, Tom, 100
Wilson, Earl, 2
Wimbledon, 28
worry, corrosion of, 54

yes-man, 148